SHAKESPEARE'S COUNTRY
IN COLOUR

SHAKESPEARE'S COUNTRY
IN COLOUR

*A Collection
of Colour Photographs*

*With an Introductory Text
and Notes on the Illustrations by*

JOAN FLEMING

LONDON
B. T. BATSFORD LTD

First Published, 1960

PRINTED IN THE NETHERLANDS
BY L. VAN LEER & CO LTD, LONDON AND AMSTERDAM
AND BOUND BY DORSTEL PRESS LTD, HARLOW, ESSEX
FOR THE PUBLISHERS
B. T. BATSFORD LTD.
4 FITZHARDINGE STREET, PORTMAN SQUARE, LONDON, W.1

CONTENTS

		Page
	List of Illustrations	6
I	The North Cotswolds	7
II	All Round Bredon Hill	18
III	The City of Worcester and Shakespeare's Villages	29
IV	Great Houses near Stratford	40
	The Illustrations	48
	Map	96

LIST OF ILLUSTRATIONS

	Page
Anne Hathaway's Cottage, Shottery, Warwickshire	49
Shakespeare's Birthplace, Stratford-upon-Avon, Warwickshire	51
Shakespeare Memorial Theatre, Stratford-upon-Avon, Warwickshire	53
Old Tramway Bridge, Stratford-upon-Avon, Warwickshire	55
Mary Arden's House at Wilmcote, Warwickshire	57
Henley-in-Arden, Warwickshire	59
Welford-on-Avon, Warwickshire	61
The River and The Seventeenth Century Bridge at Bidford, Warwickshire	63
Jephson Gardens, Leamington Spa, Warwickshire	65
Exhall, Warwickshire	67
Stoneleigh Abbey, Warwickshire	69
Compton Wynyates, Warwickshire	71
Kenilworth Castle, Warwickshire	73
Worcester Cathedral	75
Pershore Abbey, Worcestershire	77
Chaddesley Corbett, Worcestershire	79
Great Comberton, Worcestershire	81
'The Old Fleece', Bretforton, Worcestershire	83
Fladbury Ferry, Worcestershire	85
Broadway, Worcestershire	87
Landscape near Stow-on-the-Wold, Gloucestershire	89
The Church, Chipping Campden, Gloucestershire	91
The Mill, River and Abbey at Tewkesbury, Gloucestershire	93
Summer Evening at Stanton, Gloucestershire	95

I The North Cotswolds

The essence of enjoyable sightseeing is only to see what you want to see, what gives you pleasure and not simply what you are told is a must.

Very little is known about Shakespeare the man; in fact we can only be certain that those sprightly young feet have actually trodden a very small area indeed. We know, for instance, that he 'went unwillingly to school' at Stratford Grammar school and that when he 'came to wive' the two announcements of his marriage, first to Anne Whateley and next to Anne Hathaway, were made in the episcopal register at Worcester. And we can be pretty certain that he rode into Evesham market and to Henley-in-Arden and to Warwick. The rest is conjecture, legend and guesswork.

Thus the title *Shakespeare's Country* covers a very wide area indeed. For the sake of convenience it can be divided into a rough square with Kenilworth at the top right-hand corner, a straight line across the top of the square ends in Worcester. From Worcester another line is drawn to Tewkesbury. The bottom of the square crosses from Tewkesbury, through Winchcombe to Stow-on-the-Wold and straight back along the Fosse Way to Kenilworth.

Now that square is absolutely packed with delight, the little golden heart of England.

But just outside and to the South West, lie the Malvern Hills. It is hardly possible to be anywhere in the square without seeing this strange line of hills.

The Malvern Hills are one of the wonders of Europe. This ridge of seven hills, which in places achieves the status of mountain, is pre-Cambrian and amongst the oldest in the world. The hills grew, or were shot up out of the earth's surface as it cooled down, and Mount Everest was but a lad when the Malverns were well advanced in years. From level lush country through which the rivers Severn and Avon drawl, this exciting ridge of hills rises suddenly and steeply; you can walk along a footpath at the absolute crest and the ground, a foot or so on either side of the path, drops dramatically away so that you have the feeling that if you fell, there would be nothing to stop you rolling over and over down the silky grass till you reached the bottom. The sound of barking rises loud and clear from a dog outside a house so small that you might be seeing it from an aeroplane. All the country round is dominated by these hills which constantly change in character; sometimes they are an important range of distant blue mountains; sometimes foothills dozing in the sun; in winter, with snow on the northern flanks, they put up a very good imitation of Swiss Alps and, when it is going to rain, they are a dark blue and seem to have moved many miles nearer.

Celia Fiennes, a kinswoman of Lord Saye and Sele of Broughton Castle near Banbury, rode on a large white horse, side-saddle, all over England in the second half of the seventeenth century. It is said that she was the origin of the nursery rhyme:

> *Ride a cock horse to Banbury Cross*
> *To see a fine lady ride on a white horse...*

7

fine being a pun on the name Fiennes, which is pronounced *fine*. Whether or not she wore rings on her fingers or bells on her toes, she certainly had very sharp eyes, a keen sense of observation and the energy to write down her impressions of what she had seen after what must have been pretty exhausting days of riding, and we are greatly indebted to her for all sorts of homely information about the England of that time. For instance, this is what she wrote about the Malverns in or before 1696:

> *...here we enter into Worcestershire and ascend Mauborn hills or as some term them the English Alps – a ridge of hills divideing Worcestershire and Herifordshire and was formerly esteemed the [line] divideing England and Wales, Herriford, Shropshire, etc., were Weltch Countys – they are at least 2 or 3 miles up and are in a Pirrimidy fashion on the top; I rode up upon the top of the highest, from whence could discern the Country above 40 miles round, and none hills but what appeared like Burrows or Mole hills; these being so high nothing could limitt the eye but distance. Just at the bottom stands Worcester town which lookes like a large well built town of brick and stone, I was not in it; on the one side of this high Ridge of Hills lies Worcester Oxford and Glocestershire etc appears in Plaines Enclosures Woods and Rivers and many great Hills tho' to this they appeare low; on the other side is Herrifordshire which appear like a Country off Gardens and Orchards, the whole Country being very full of fruite trees etc, it lookes like nothing else, the apple pear trees etc., are so thick even in their corn fields and hedgerows.*

> *The descent is as long and steep in some places as its riseing was; thence to a Relations house, my uncle John Fiennes and his son, New House, 20 mile from Parshur (Pershore) which I rode all in one day in June.*

Her fine disregard for spelling and punctuation make her descriptions no less graphic.

From the top of the Malvern Hills, the tiny ridge to the South East is the North Western end of the Cotswold Hills and from Broadway, which lies at the foot of these hills, on the edge of the Vale of Evesham, this rise from the valley to the summit of the hill called Fish Hill is no mean incline. It is part of the main road from Worcester to London. In the Worcester County Records in 1752 it was ordered 'that no common waggoner or carrier shall take for carrying any goods to or from Bewdley (the barge port) to London the sum of more than 7s. per cwt till further order'. And again in 1752 'that every waggon or other carriage drawn up from the signe of the White Hart (now The Lygon Arms) Broadway to the top of the hill, so far as in the county of Worcester, may be drawn with ten horses if the owner shall think proper'. It is interesting to note that an order follows immediately: 'Ditto, up the Malvern Hill, with seven.'

Near the top of the hill a gatepost can still be seen, upon which are the words: *Shutt off two horses here.*

The county boundary of Worcester is eccentric and variable; Broadway is a small peninsula of Worcestershire with Gloucestershire almost surrounding it. At present the division to the East between Worcestershire and Gloucestershire comes exactly at the summit of the hill where there is an old stone-built hostelry with a stone outside staircase immediately opposite a newly-built petrol station. When the latter was being constructed recently, a number of interesting weapons and relics of Ancient Britain were found and many fossils. There is, indeed, a legend that Fish Hill got its name from the fossil of a fish which was found there.

Round the Fish Inn, the land is bare and greatly quarried, but these quarries yield a splendid harvest of fossils from the smallest of shells to large cockle-shell-like stones called ammonites after the horn of Jupiter (Ammon).

Broadway itself is best seen in the early morning or late at night when the traffic has abated. There is a variety of opinions about this mile-long village, but taken in a good mood, it is incredibly beautiful; on a stormy evening against a dark grey sky with the dark blue hills as a background, the houses reflect an unearthly golden glow which is unforgettable. Seen from a little way up the hill on a clear frosty morning with the smoke from the newly-lighted fires rising briskly it lies like a small treasure trove of gold and platinum in a pale grey and silvery brown setting. And at dusk on a late autumnal evening, when it is not quite dark enough to draw the curtains, though the lights are being turned on and the fires made up, there is an enchanting smell of wet limestone and wood smoke and you can hear nearby the hounds coming back home, the peremptory shouts from the huntsmen and the padding of many wet paws; then, walking down the village street, you may feel that this is the epitome of English life under an English sky and possibly, in the unreal light of that time of day, you may feel that Shakespeare himself saw it looking pretty much the same.

On the road from Broadway to Winchcombe, there are several entrancing villages of which the most famous is Stanway, which has a fine Elizabethan hall with what used to be a formal garden rising to a viewpoint on the hillside amongst the Wellingtonias and other cultivated trees. There is an interesting gatehouse attributed to Inigo Jones and a beautifully restored tithe barn, now the village hall.

A hundred yards or so outside the village, at a strangely quiet tree-shaded crossroads, is a War Memorial of the 1914–1918 War.

Men of Stanway

it says:

For their Tomb they have an Altar
For Lamentation Memory
And for Pity Praise.

It bears the names of the thirteen Men of Stanway who died in that war, amongst whom are two sets of brothers, the brothers Buggins, and the brothers Charteris, the elder, Hugo Francis Charteris, Lord Elcho, being heir to the Earldom of Wemyss and March.

The charming memorial was planned by his widow and his mother; the stone plinth was built by a local mason called Grimmet, and the steps are in the shape of a Tudor Rose. The words are from Simonides' epitaph on *The Greek dead at Thermo-*

pylae and were carved personally on the stone by the late Eric Gill. The bronze figure of St. George and the Dragon was done by Alexander Fisher and was chosen because Lord Elcho was killed on St. George's day, April 23rd (1916), incidentally the day celebrated as Shakespeare's birthday.

By far the least well-known of these villages is Buckland; it is so tiny that it is hardly more than a hamlet but still has the status of village by reason of its church and manor house which stand huddled shoulder to shoulder. The church is almost untouched; there is a fine sample of seventeenth-century oak panelling with tester heads and hat pegs; fifteenth-century glass, tiles and a finely embroidered pall. Round the walls are traces of the stone bench; when it was the only form of seating provided the congregation knelt or stood but the feeble and the elderly sat on the seat, and it is said that this is the origin of the phrase *the weak go to the wall*. The church stands on a hillock and the village is in a fold of the hills. The rectory, it is said, was at one time a rest-house for pilgrims from all over England who walked to Hailes Abbey; it has a fifteenth-century hall open to the rafters and some windows with the original coloured glass.

Hailes Abbey belongs to the National Trust and is well worth a visit, not so much for what there is to see, which is practically nothing, but to sense the wonderful atmosphere of peace. The thousands of prayers that have been said for three centuries by thousands of pilgrims must have made their mark because there is no more tranquil place. And so far there is not an inch of discarded orange peel to distract the eye from the felicitous arrangement of trees which show the lay-out of the old abbey.

King John's second son, Richard of Cornwall, was an ambitious young man whose activities in France earned him the title of Duke of Aquitaine, and in 1257 he pleased the Electors of the Holy Roman Empire so much that he was crowned King of the Romans which, one gathers, was more or less an honorary title. Returning from France, he was shipwrecked in a great storm in the Channel and, in thanks for his delivery, he founded the Abbey of St. Mary, for the Cistercian Order, on land that his father had given him at Hailes in Gloucestershire. It was knocked up in five years, which may be the reason why it was knocked down so thoroughly some three centuries later. There was a magnificent party for the dedication with the King (Henry III) and the Queen of England at the ceremony.

Some twenty-five years later, Richard's son Edmund, was given a sample of the Holy Blood by the Patriarch of Jerusalem; he gave it to Hailes Abbey where it was installed in a specially-built tabernacle behind the High Altar in the presence of two abbots at the Feast of the Exaltation of the Holy Cross in 1270.

It became the fashion to visit Hailes and soon there were miracles of healing. 'As sure as God's in Gloucestershire' people said and all the year round thousands of pilgrims poured into Hailes along the Pilgrim's Way. No one will doubt that many miracles of healing did take place because it is, of course, the faith that heals, not the object of the faith. With the swing of the pendulum against the Catholics, however, scepticism began to seep in. The Holy Relic was sent to the High Sheriff of Gloucestershire who, with Bishop Latimer of Worcester, examined it and delivered a scathing judgement to the effect that it was merely *unctuous gumme couloured* and on November 24th 1539 it was ceremoniously burned.

The tiny church, now the parish church, is outside National Trust property but is essentially part of the abbey. It was built in 1130, long before the abbey was thought of and, when the great new abbey was erected, it was handed over and probably used as a guest-house chapel as it stands beside the site of the entrance gate. It is quite unspoilt and charming. The pews are those made by the Puritan carpenter who, under the Commonwealth, probably made the table for the Lord's Supper which still stands upon the original altar stone. The rood screen and the pulpit are excellent, as is all the woodwork, including a mediaeval carving of Saint Cecilia, the patron saint of light. Under the chancel windows can be seen heraldic emblems in places on the walls dating from the thirteenth century, and a number of Norman-British shields commemorate the royal visits to Hailes. Much of the floor is flagged with tiles which came from the abbey. There is an open black-and-white timber roof and the bell tower is timber and plaster.

Outside it is so quiet; the custodian of the abbey grounds sits in his hut awaiting custom; the swifts swing down in formation, screaming with pleasure. The peace is not that of emptiness but of not-there-ness, which is different and beyond understanding.

The hills above Hailes and Winchcombe differ remarkably from the Malverns and Bredon; they are rounded and gentle and fold in upon each other affectionately. The new electric grid system from Gloucester strides across the breast-like contours trailing the heavy cables as lightly as a spider throws out its web. Postlip Hall is an Elizabethan manor in the traditional style. Now privately owned, it is hidden from the road in a dimple of the hills. It has a tiny Norman chapel. Below, hidden from view from practically anywhere, is Postlip Mill, a Victorian edifice which must be the most beautifully situated Mill in England; where they make blotting paper.

Winchcombe itself is an attractive old wool town. Behind the wall over which great branches of ilex hang, in the centre of the town are the scant remains of another abbey which was torn down by Cromwell. This abbey's claim to fame was the body of a boy-saint, Kenelm. There seems to be no reason as to why Kenelm should have been canonized other than that, when seven years old, he was murdered in a thicket by his sister who was possibly a psychopath and about whom many a gory legend rages. However, the abbey did quite nicely out of the grave of little Saint Kenelm as many pilgrims called at Winchcombe on their way to and from Hailes.

The church, built in the lavish style from the money made from wool, is late Perpendicular with an enormous golden cock on the tower. Some of the gargoyles are quite deliciously revolting.

There are some delightful houses in the town. The George is an old posting inn with an original gallery but is a great deal older than the days of posting; it was used by the wealthier pilgrims on their way to Hailes.

Half a mile from Winchcombe is Sudeley Castle, now privately owned but open to the public at stated times. Hardly any of the original castle remains but it is of great interest historically, being closely connected with the Seymours of whom one,

11

Jane, was Henry VIII's wife, coming between Anne Boleyn and Anne of Cleves and dying in childbirth after less than a year as Queen of England.

Sudeley belonged to the Seymours, and Jane's young brother Thomas was a courtier who married Katherine Parr, the only one of Henry VIII's wives who succeeded in surviving him.

This last wife of Henry VIII crops up over and over again in this part of the world; her arms may be seen in many tiny churches, the manors in which they are situated having been part of the Queen's dowry.

Katherine Parr comes down through history as being a woman of charm and character; as step-mother of the young Princess Elizabeth, she was evidently kind and understanding. The Princess got into some trouble about the age of twelve for which her young brother King Edward banished her from court for a short time. Katherine, now the Dowager Queen, evidently took part in the Princess's restoration to favour because the Princess gave her a New Year's gift in 1545 of a book of French poems in the front of which she wrote: 'To our most noble and vertuous Queen Katerine, Elizabeth her humble daughter wisheth perpetual felicity and everlasting joy.'

One cannot help feeling Katherine Parr was a thoroughly nice woman. Towards the end of her pregnancy, she came to Sudeley Castle where she gave birth to a child and died herself a week later from septicaemia. She lies buried at Sudeley in a vault around which Sir Gilbert Scott has built a private chapel. The whole castle was restored by him; the situation is delightful and unique and, from a distance, it is almost beautiful, brooding over the little town in the way a mediaeval castle should.

It is a lovely drive up over the hills between Winchcombe and Stow-on-the-Wold, with many places of interest on the way: the Swells and the Slaughters, Upper and Lower, are typical small villages, all built in the same miraculous grey-gold stone, with streams and tiny bridges, churches and manor houses, tithe barns and preaching or butter crosses.

The Manor of Snowshill was part of Katherine Parr's dowry when she married the King. There is a Jacobean manor house with Queen Anne additions, which belongs to the National Trust and attracts many visitors to view the collections of curios and antiques arranged there by the late owner. The guide books might well describe Snowshill Manor as 'a stone-built Jacobean house beautifully situated on the hillside with a charming garden, and packed with *things*'.

The church is not old, but the formation of the village, sheltering itself from the North and East winds, perched high above the Vale of Evesham with the cottages and the Manor arranged round the open space on which the church stands, is unique and attractive. In one of the cottages, the sewing machine was invented.

The nicest towns and villages in the Cotswolds are those self-contained, quietly brooding little places which seem hardly to notice the traffic which flashes through. Stow-on-the-Wold is one of these places and Bourton-on-the-Hill is another.

In the south-westernmost corner of our square is Stow-on-the-Wold, where was the first settlement in England known to have been occupied by pre-historic man.

If Stow-on-the-Wold has retained its integrity, it has also kept the dickens of a draught.

the inhabitants quote proudly. For a wool town, the church is not remarkable, but the town itself is the perfect example of a small prosperous country town. The market square is surrounded by houses in the same grey-gold stone, roofed with the old Cotswold tiles, moss and lichengrown. Though built on the Fosse Way, with the traffic racing through, it has retained a peacefulness which is remarkable. Celia Fiennes, in her careless way, calls it *Stow-on-the-Old;* she could, of course, not merely be missing out the *W* but referring to it as she may have heard it referred to: Stow-on-the-Old (Roman Road), that is, on the Fosse Way which the Romans built from Exeter to Lincoln and which is still, for a great deal of its length, used as a public highway.

Indeed, a mile or so from Stow, its old bones are exposed in a carefully preserved spot beside the tarmac, where the original road surface can be seen clearly.

Moreton-in-the-Marsh is the next town northwards along the Fosse Way from Stow. It is on the main line from London to Worcester and The Cathedrals Express, which takes exactly two hours from Paddington, stops there by an arrangement which was originally arrived at by the lord of the Manor of Batsford who allowed the Great Western Railway to cross his land on condition that the best train of the day should stop there in perpetuity. It always does.

Celia Fiennes calls it Moreton-Hindmost; it is not easy to see quite why; for present-day inhabitants of the district it is Moreton-Foremost. She says: '...thence to Morton Hindmost in Gloucestershire to a Relations house, My Uncle Richard Fiennes widdow; a neate little stone built town, good Innes for the travellers, being the road from London to Worcester and Herrifford and Wales.' There are still excellent inns for the traveller. The Roman road runs straight through the main street which is very wide and bordered by charming stone-built houses. Many of the trees which grew along either side have been taken down and replaced by small wisps which may one day be trees. The Town Hall stands, like a rude word, in the centre of a wide expanse of asphalt which now replaces the grassy verge, but the old lock-up with the curfew bell still exists, bent and crippled, by the petrol station opposite the Town Hall. There are numerous concrete lamp posts from which, in the winter, flows a blaze of orange sodium light, by which one can certainly see on a dark night.

A mile to the East of Moreton is the Four Shires Stone, where Worcestershire, Oxfordshire, Gloucestershire and Warwickshire meet. This was once an important place for criminals of all kinds as jurisdiction for each of the four counties began and ended at this point and they could escape arrest for quite some time by dodging in and out of the various territories. A small uncompromising monument, it was knocked down recently by a lorry but re-erected. No one notices it much now but, at one time, it must have been quite an important land-mark for travellers; Celia Fiennes mentioned it twice and in her day it probably stood out importantly in the midst of what was no doubt marshy and rather desolate country.

Two miles West of Moreton, on the Worcester road, the land rises steeply to the Five Mile Drive across the top end of the Cotswolds to Fish Hill, which, as stated previously, descends sharply to the Vale of Evesham. On the Eastern slope, over-looking Moreton, is the charming village of Bourton-on-the-Hill. A long flat road, along which the traffic puts on speed, leads suddenly to the village which does not start until the road rises really rapidly, so that most travellers are so intent on taking the hill in fine style, possibly in top gear, that they do not notice the village which, in the opinion of many, is the most delightful in that part of the Cotswolds.

It has a housing estate which is one of the country's prides and bus-loads of wel-fare workers from all over the world are brought to see the stone-built houses with their tiny gardens which fit so perfectly into the scene below the mediaeval village.

Bourton House is a show place and was visited by the late Queen Mary. It is connected with Sir Thomas Overbury and thereby hangs a tale, but there are varied opinions as to how close was his connection with the house. It has been said that he was born there but that seems to be in doubt. Sir Thomas Overbury is an interesting character about whom one would like to know a good deal more. He was born in 1581 and went to Queen's College, Oxford, where he read Law, being called to the Middle Temple. Somehow or other he got across Robert Carr, Earl of Somerset, who was his patron, on the subject of Carr's marriage with the divorced Countess of Essex. He was banged into the Tower, where the malice of the Countess followed him and he was slowly poisoned, dying at the age of thirty-two. Though Robert Carr and his wife were convicted of the murder, they were reprieved, in fact pardoned, though four others connected with the murder were hanged. Francis Bacon conducted the case for the Crown and whether the Earl and Countess were pardoned because there was some doubt as to their guilt or whether it was merely their social position which in-fluenced the situation is a moot point and one which is still argued vigorously amongst historians. It is one of the Great Unsolved Mysteries of all time. Sir Thomas Overbury, in his short life, wrote some rather charming poetry and his *Miscellaneous Works in Verse and Prose* were actually re-issued and edited by the French poet Rim-baud in 1856.

In the early morning, Bourton-on-the-Hill gets the full sun; it springs into golden and silver life and, seen against a pale blue winter sky, it is breath-taking, its cottages hugging the road right up to the top of the hill, the church in the middle and the big square manor house, standing a little back from the road, beyond the church. The road here is narrow and so steep that it needs careful negotiation and the car driver cannot possibly see it with any degree of comfort. One must either park the car at the bottom and walk up or park the car at the top and walk down, all of which seem to be too much for present-day drivers because no tourists are seen staring spell-bound at this enchanting village.

Blockley is another small and delightful town by-passed entirely by the tourist. Two miles or so from Bourton-on-the-Hill and Chipping Campden, it is almost com-pletely hidden until one comes suddenly upon it, first seeing the top of the church tower.

This little town has a character of its own which is rather surprising. There are no sharp roofs built at the angle of fifty degrees which the stone tiles require A-shaped gables. The roofs of the flat-fronted Georgian houses are covered in Welsh grey slates, but the stone from which the houses are built is still the same golden-yellow. There is plenty of water, with streams everywhere and a small reservoir in the open space in the centre.

This strong source of water was put to good use at the beginning of the industrial revolution; many small mills were built for the mysterious process known locally as *throusting* raw silk which was carted over from Coventry, and returned to that town to be made into ribbon when the *throusting* was completed. With the invention of improved machinery, the whole proceeding was discontinued but, during that comparatively short period, Blockley became a flourishing small industrial town, with several rows of stone-built houses of great charm built on sharply rising ground overlooking the church and mill pool.

In Southern Spain the silk-worms are still churning out their silk but the inhabitants of Blockley couldn't care less; they now go in bus loads to Redditch, where they make needles for sewing with the silk which was their forefathers' livelihood.

This part of the country cannot be left without mention of the great house of Sezincote, privately owned but sometimes open to the public. It is built on the hillside above Moreton, on a level with Bourton-on-the-Hill, hidden by carefully planted trees. It is constructed of limestone, but in a style which used to be described as *fantastick*. Horace Walpole led the fashion for *fantastick* houses with his *Strawberry Hill* and the owner of Sezincote went a good deal further and re-furbished his house in an even more elaborate style reminiscent of the newer Taj Mahal. It is said that Prinny, or George, Prince of Wales, took one look at Sezincote and dashed off to find an architect who would convert his villa at Brighton to a similar style, hence Brighton Pavilion.

Looking again Stratford-wards, we come to Dover's Hill, above the attractive village of Weston Subedge to the West and Chipping Campden to the East.

Dover's
Antient Meeting
On Thursday in Whit Week
On that highly renowned and universally
admired spot
called
Dover's Hill
near
Chipping Campden, Glos
The sports will commence
with a grand match of backswords
for a purse of guineas
to be played by 9 or 7 men on a side
Each side must appear in the ring
by 3 o'clock in the afternoon
or 15s each pair will be given
for so many as will play

WRESTLING
for belts and other prizes
Also
jumping in bags and dancing
and a jingling Match for 10.6d.
As well as divers others of celebrated
Cotswold and Olympic games
for which this annual
meeting has been
famed for centuries.

(circa 1804)

A certain Mr Robert Dover, a man of jovial disposition and a sportsman, selected a flat strip of land at the top of a hill for the annual holding of sport and games at Whitsuntide which were begun in the first decade of the seventeenth century and held for two hundred and fifty years, with a break during the Commonwealth when Cromwell laid the icy hand of disapproval on the revelries. The idea was an immediate success and Dover's young friend Endymion Porter, patron of poets and a member of the Long Parliament, obtained from King James I some of his cast-off clothing, including a plumed hat which Robert Dover wore at the games.

The sports were commonly called the *Whitsun-ale* or *Ale* and were held on the Thursday and Friday in Whit week. They included football, skittles, quoits, shovel board, cudgell and single stick, bull baiting, cock-fighting, bowling, leaping, dancing, wrestling, pitching the bar, horse racing (introduced later), ringing of bells, and jumping in sacks, etc.

Dover himself was astonished at the way people came from as far away as twenty miles and more and his name became famous. It may be that the Whitsun-ale was held many years before in the neighbourhood and that Robert Dover, coming into a new district merely revived the old custom. In his day they were held with great decorum but later on they deteriorated, becoming very rowdy indeed in the Georges' time. With the coming of the railway, crowds of what was then described as *riff raff* came out from the industrial areas and the behaviour at the top of Dover's Hill became such a scandal that the Vicar of Weston Subedge said it would be impossible to describe the demoralizing effect the games had upon his parish. He prompted a Bill for the enclosure of the space, which became Law in 1850, and the games were discontinued.

It is said that Shakespeare frequently attended the games and it is from his observations there that he wrote the wrestling scene in *As You Like It*.

There are a few copies of a small, much-valued book in existence called *Annalia Dubrensia* which is a collection of what can only be called doggerel of a very good-natured kind, written in honour and praise of the popular Robert Dover by various friends, two of whom were professional poets, Ben Jonson and Michael Drayton.

One Francis Izod, Gent. of Stanton bursts into enthusiastic praise and ends:

Therefore my Sonnett I will period; and so end
Whispring a word or two in private to my friend
Achilles name had bin interr'd with him (brave Dover)
Had not queint Homers muse so queintly nam'd it over.

And Mr William Durham of Willersey ends his verses:

Thus shall they daily sing, sit, hatch a laugh
And to thy health (brave Dover) freely quaffe.

The verses of Mr William Ambrose, headmaster of Evesham Grammar School from 1620 to 1642 could hardly be worse:

This Epitaph his noble Urne shall cover,
COTSWOLD'S ETERNIZER, ROBERT DOVER
Whose Anagran by after ages, read,
Ecchoes his Fame thus: O most rare! True bred.
    MASTER ROBERT DOVER
      ANAGRAM
O most rare! True bred.

II All Round Bredon Hill

To leave Broadway and drive westwards along the Evesham road towards the Malverns is to leave behind the Cotswold Hills, yellow limestone and steep-tiled roofs. The Vale of Evesham is very different country; the earth is often richly red, the houses are mostly built of mellowed red brick and there are acres and acres of orchards stretching away into distant Herefordshire.

WICKHAMFORD, the signpost some three miles from Broadway seems to insist. But there is really no need for emphasis because we would be going there anyway. Wickhamford is the Mecca of most Americans who are interested in their forefathers.

Alas! some of the cottages peering out from overhanging thatch are rather ominously what Osbert Lancaster calls *stockbroker Tudor;* some have thatched *Tudor* garages. But the ochre-washed farmhouse on the right looks more promising and the manor house and church beside the stream in the quiet corner where the road has become a mere lane are not only worth coming to but evoke cries of delight.

The manor house is everything that the minds calls up at the thought of Elizabethan manors. It is built of soft pinkish brick and stone, and is half-timbered. It stands, modest and unselfconscious, looking out from large latticed windows with cool greenish glass across smooth lawns with a background of trees to the little lake upon which grows a satisfying crust of water lilies. At one time carp for the house would be stocked in the lake. There is a great fat stone pigeon house which could house hundreds of pigeons. It is said that to eat nothing but pigeon meat for a month causes madness but there is no doubt that pigeons were a large item of food in upper class houses at certain times in the year; nearly every large dwelling has its own pigeon house.

This enchanting place was the home of Penelope Washington who was closely related to the great Washingtons of Sulgrave Manor near Banbury. A plain stone slab, rather worn and inscribed in Latin, in the floor of the chancel in the church, is enthusiastic about Penelope; it reads:

> *Sacred to the memory of Penelope,*
> *daughter of that most distinguished*
> *and renowned soldier Colonel Henry*
> *Washington. He was descended from*
> *Sir William Washington Kt., of the*
> *county of Northampton, who was high*
> *in favour with those illustrious*
> *princes and best of kings, Charles*
> *the First and Second, on account of*
> *his gallant and successful military*
> *achievements both in England and in*
> *Ireland: he married Elizabeth, of*
> *Westwood, a family of untarnished*

loyalty and patriotism. Sprung from
such famous ancestry, Penelope was
a diligent and devout worshipper of God;
she was the great consolation of her
mother (her only surviving parent);
to the sick and needy she was an excep-
tionally ready and generous benefactress.
Humble and chaste, and wedded to Christ
alone, from this transitory life she
departed to her Spouse. February 27
Anno Domini 1697.

It sounds much more important in Latin. The grave stone is headed with her arms; the stars and stripes which were the inspiration of the American flag of today, are easily discernible. Poor Penelope; was she a little overpowered by her splendid ancestry? Hers is a humble position in the chancel. And she was not demanding about her armorial bearings; there are only three stars and two stripes!

Above this simple stone are the really splendid marble effigies of the Sandys family into which her mother married, as her second marriage. Sir Samuel Sandys and his wife Mercy had four sons and six daughters, all of whom kneel below their parents, the four eldest girls wearing adorable little hats. He was the son of 'the famous prelate Edwyn Archbishop of York' and himself a Dean of the Arches, which meant being a lay judge at the *Court of the Arches* – the charming title of the ecclesiastical court of appeal for the province of Canterbury, formerly held at the church of St. Mary-le-Bow, so-named from the arches that supported its steeple in 1297.

Sir Edwyn Sandys and his wife Penelope lie in the adjoining niche; they had three daughters, hatless but one wearing a small cap, and four sons. There may have been an epidemic of some kind which killed both father and son as they both died in the same year, the father on September 2nd and the son on September 23rd, 1626.

To most people Simon de Montfort is a dull character about whom it is important to know that he was killed in the battle of Evesham, which was the last and decisive battle of the Wars of the Roses, the euphemistic title given to the bloody Barons' War. Simon de Montfort was a Frenchman, Count de Montfort-l'Amaury who was given the courtesy title of Earl of Leicester. He and one of his sons were killed fighting and lie buried under the High Altar of the old Abbey.

The precise events which led up to the battle of Evesham in 1265 involve a great deal of history, but the actual battle took place between Simon de Montfort's army and an army of Welsh barons of the Marches (Edward I being at Simon de Montfort's side at Evesham). Owing to the geography of the Avon which takes a decisive loop at Evesham, the reinforcements which de Montfort's army were expecting did not turn up and for three hours there was a terrible massacre in the fields between the Abbey and the river. Eighteen barons were killed, with a hundred and sixty knights and four thousand foot soldiers in that small area. The monks of the Abbey recorded that a great cloud covered the August sky and a thunderstorm raged.

Today the Abbey park, beside the river, is a scene of absolute peace. All that remains of the Abbey is the Bell Tower and the old timbered Almonry. There is a modern monument to Simon de Montfort and an obelisk marks the exact spot where he is supposed to have fallen.

A legend arose around him and for many years pilgrimages were made to Evesham, the scene of the fearful battle and the death of a hero and sainted martyr of liberty and justice. Historians are of the opinion that the outcome of the battle of Evesham made an impression of enduring value to the nation.

So much history was made in this small square of Shakespeare's country. It may be because this countryside was cultivated and built upon when large areas of the rest of England were still forest, wild and marshy. Elizabeth the Great made frequent appearances with her train on visits to country houses all over Gloucestershire, Worcestershire, Oxfordshire and Warwickshire. Shakespeare's sovereign seems to have been particularly fond of the country through which the Avon and the Severn run.

Within a few square miles there are three of our best cathedrals; two splendid Abbey Churches, at Malvern and Tewkesbury; dozens of small village churches, some of great antiquity and most of them with effigies of members of the families who helped to make England famous. Three great battles were fought, at Evesham, Tewkesbury and Worcester. The city and the country around were strongly Royalist in the Civil Wars. And the world's greatest poet was born, married, had children and lived the latter years of his life here.

Catesby and the instigators of the Gunpowder Plot are reported to have met and discussed plans in at least seven large country houses. Catesby had relatives at Lypiatt Park, near Stroud, where he spent much time, and it was, of course, he who was the chief organiser of this plot, surely, the greatest flop in history, though poor little Guy Fawkes is the one whose effigy will be burned till the end of time.

After Elizabeth had died and James VI of Scotland had sought the help of the Catholics in his claim to the throne, Catholicism took a new hold and the Bishop of Gloucester returned an impressive list of recusants from his diocese, mentioning people living in no less than fifty-five villages in the country between the Cotswolds and the Malverns, some of them being from the delightful small villages which lie around the foot of Bredon Hill.

There is something very special about Bredon and those who live within sight of it love it and are passionately anxious to save it from the awful fate of Box Hill, around and on which the populace sweat and roll and gambol on every possible occasion. It has therefore been made impossible to travel over the top of Bredon in a car, and anybody who wants to see the world from there must park their car in an orderly manner and simply use their feet, an exercise which is becoming less and less popular.

A walk round and over Bredon Hill must be one of the most pleasurable and satisfying in England. The word *serendipity*, which was coined by Horace Walpole, sounds pedantic but has been popularised by the owners of a coffee bar-cum-antique shop in New York which they have called by that name. The precise meaning is 'the faculty of making happy and unexpected discoveries by accident' and if ever there was a *Serendipity Walk* it must be this.

Without specifying exactly where, it can be stated that there is a cherry orchard near the top so glorious in the spring that you wonder whether, perhaps, you have been accidentally killed and this is heaven. It is just as wonderful in July when the cherries are hanging ripe and it has the playful look of a newly-decorated Christmas tree. There are pedlars' tracks leading across smooth silky grass in open spaces from which the whole world seems to be spread at your feet. There is a tiny Gothic castle simply smothered in roses; a group of oolitic stones (so called from its fish-roe-like formation); a stone cider press; several old butter crosses, or preaching crosses, as some people believe them to be; innumerable tiny black and white cottages of great antiquity; and a variety of wild flowers. There is a British Camp which was one of a chain of forts stretching across England. There are many fossils to be found and Roman coins too, if you are lucky. Nash, in his *History of Worcestershire*, states that a prehistoric toad was found alive twenty feet below the ground in a kind of smooth nest which it had made for itself, like the inside of an oyster shell. He records that it lived for several hours.

There are some who sense, at the top of Bredon, an eerie feeling which someone has described as a *strong smell of Druid*. The Druids were not elderly gentlemen with enhampering robes and long beards and rheumy eyes but a secret society of proven warriors. The Celtic word Druid means oak-man, and their sacred year began with the budding of the oak and ended with the falling of its leaf. The mistletoe which grew on the oak was the keynote of the mystic rites which they performed; and on St. John's Eve, which is Midsummer's Eve, the golden bough had to be cut with a golden knife and caught in a white cloth before it touched the ground. Sacrifices were made on their sacred altars which were called *dolmens* and it is said that the Bambury Stone on Bredon, one of the oolitic rocks, formed like the hull of a ship, was used as a dolmen by the Druids. In the main, their activities were carried out in their sacred groves of oak trees and, though the hanging woods at the top of Bredon are not essentially of oak, it is evident that, on Bredon, trees can and do grow profusely at nine hundred feet.

All this and a Folly, too!

And if you are not interested in serendipity, you can enjoy Bredon, as A. E. Housman did when he wrote:

> *Here of a Sunday morning*
> *My love and I would lie*
> *And see the coloured counties*
> *And hear the larks so high*
> *About us in the sky.*

Each of the Bredon villages has its own flavour, its own individuality, its own particular bit of history, and it is not easy to decide which one to write about. Bredon itself, perhaps, is the most famous, with one of the best tithe barns in England and some fine timberframed houses.

At Bredon's Norton, America's best-known suffragette, Victoria Woodhall Martin, lived for a time; she stood as a candidate for the office of President of the U.S.A. Americans will be more likely to know how near to the office she came.

A Parliamentary soldier, passing through Bricklehampton, was so charmed by it that, after the battle of Worcester, when the Parliamentarians were successful, he applied for permission to purchase half an acre of land in the village to build a house house upon. The lord of the Manor refused his application but the soldier applied to the Sessions and leave was granted.

Elmley Castle was the scene of a big family row. The village is named after the castle, once the home of the D'Abitots and the Beauchamps, now a ruin. Park House, adjoining the church, now stands empty, but was lived in by the Savages for several centuries. There is a splendid memorial in the church to William Savage, who died in 1616, his son Giles and his daughter-in-law. Father, son and daughter-in-law lie side by side, carved in beautiful luminous marble. The daughter holds a baby, wrapped so tightly in swaddling clothes that it looks like a log of wood, but it has been described as the best effigy of a baby carved in marble in existence. The four sons kneeling at the foot of the monument are in excellent condition but this extremely fine monument is overpowered by a memorial which is a rather splendid example of English Baroque. It stands against the wall, a grim warning to the socially over-ambitious. It is a monument to Thomas, Lord Coventry, who, in his dotage, married the housekeeper's niece. When he died in 1699, his widow had this elaborate and expensive monument made which contains a short statement as to her own ancestory and space left for her own name and date of her death, to be inscribed when the time came. She sent it over to Croome d'Abitot, where the Earl is buried, evidently lacking the courage to go with it herself, and there it was greeted by the then Earl of Coventry, her step-son, to the effect that 'only over his dead body', etc., etc. The equipage was turned round and sent smartly back to Elmley Castle together with some hard words from the Earl with reference to his step-mother's lineage. She then had it squeezed into the church at Elmley Castle, because there was nowhere else to put it, and had the words inscribed:

> *Reader build thou thy tomb while yet thou livest*
> *If fortune hath not given thee a spouse*

into which a world of meaning can be read.

The countess, however, had nothing to grumble about: she soon recovered from her grief and chagrin and married William Savage, who had been on her side and thoroughly sympathetic throughout, and, one presumes, lived happily ever after.

Queen Elizabeth, of course, stayed at Elmley Castle and the inn shows a modern sign with her portrait on one side and the scene of her arrival on the other.

Croome Court was the once-splendid home of the Coventrys. It was founded at the time of Henry VI by John Coventry, Lord Mayor of London in succession to Dick Whittington. The Earldom was conferred upon the uncle of the third Baron who succeeded in 1687. The third Earl, succeeding at the age of eight, died two years later; the ninth Earl succeeded as a child of five and lived to be ninety-one and was greatly loved and respected.

Lancelot Brown, or Capability Brown, as he was called, who designed the gardens at Blenheim, was employed to beautify the gardens at Croome which, apparently, he did very successfully, as a fashionable magazine of 1792 fell over itself declaring a trifle ambiguously: 'If there be a spot upon the habitable globe to make a deathbed terrible, it is Lord Coventry's at Croome...'

On arrival there now, there doesn't seem to be a garden at all. Nuns and dozens of small lively boys in grey shorts and blue shirts enliven the rather grim frontage; it is at present a junior school for mentally retarded Catholic boys, the senior branch being a mile or so away at Besford Court (where it is said Queen Elizabeth also stayed). But on looking round, a certain gracious arrangement of trees such as one has seen at Blenheim can be recognised; though there is no water, bridge or view-point, there is a small unobtrusive urn on a pedestal which is dedicated

To the Memory of
LANCELOT BROWN
who, by the powers of his inimitable and creative genius,
formed this garden scene out of
A MORASS

It was a Countess of Coventry who complained that she wanted a view-point and the nearest spot that could be found upon which one could be erected was thirty miles away, on the top of Broadway Hill. This is so far distant that it cannot be seen from the house at all and, even in those days, when the surrounding trees had not grown up, a bonfire had to be lighted at the top of the hill on the proposed site in order to assure the Earl that it could, in fact, be seen.

The private chapel at Croome was removed to a clearing on rising ground a little way from the house. There is a very simple approach to it, through an orchard, and the doors have to be kept shut to prevent the cows entering, but inside the church is far from simple. The chancel is jammed with monuments which appear to be trying to emulate certain effects seen in St. Peter's, Rome. The Baron Coventry who died in 1687 is seen in an attitude of supplication; lying partly raised on one arm, he is lifting the other hand towards a Hebe-like female in flowing robes, who is looking away in haughty disdain. His coronet is perched upon his head at a ridiculous angle. The church itself was designed by the same Lancelot Brown who seems to have been better at designing gardens.

Pershore, which is the nearest town to Croome, lies on the road between Evesham and Worcester, a historic road along which nearly everybody who is anybody, in history, has passed at one time. The old bridge over the Avon still stands by the main road and must have been crossed many a time by Will Shakespeare. Pershore itself is a delightful small town with houses on the street whose gardens run down to the river at the back. It is famous for its very fine plums. It has many charming Regency houses, and one particularly attractive hotel where the coaches stopped on the last stage from London to Worcester. It is almost certain that Prince Charles Stuart, afterwards Charles II, stayed at Pershore, probably several times, and that his peronal charm appealed to the townsfolk. When Cromwell's soldiers were billeted in the town before the battle of Worcester, they were treated very coldly, particularly by the women, and, for years afterwards, and sometimes even now, it was known as *Pershore Godelpus* (God help us!).

Pershore had its Benedictine Abbey and the remains of the Abbey Church are well worth a visit if only for the roof vaulting; but there are many other relics of interest.

A fair has been held annually since permission was first granted by Henry III and used to take place in the churchyard. There is an old Worcestershire saying that the cuckoo is never heard 'before Tenbury Fair (on April 20th) or after Pershore Fair (on June 26th)'.

Celia Fiennes passed through the town several times and each time found a new way of spelling it: Pusha, Parshur and Persher.

Round the other side of Bredon Hill is Upton-upon-Severn, an old barge-port about which Celia says: '...thence to Upton where we pass on a large bridge over the fine river Severn, which runs from Worcester and to Glocester, Shrewsbury and to Bristol where it runns into the Sea: in some places its very broad some miles over, but here no broader than the Thames at Staines, it affords good fish, Salmon and severall sorts besides; I think this River does not ebb and flow so farre into the land.'

She had evidently not heard of the great Severn bore which, with the neap tides at certain times of year, rises, a great enveloping wave, and sweeps up the river for many miles. In the time of Celia Fiennes, it was uncontrolled and flooded the land for thirty miles and more round.

In *Henry VI*, Act III, Scene 1 at Bangor; Hotspur, Worcester, Mortimer and Owen Glendower are together when Mortimer says:

> *The archdeacon hath divided it*
> *Into three limits very equally*
> *England from Trent and Severn hitherto*
> *By South and East is to my part assigned:*
> *All Westward, Wales beyond the Severn shore*
> *And all the fertile lands within that bound*
> *To Owen Glendower: and, dear coz, to you*
> *The remnant Northward...*

But Hotspur complains bitterly about his share:

> *See how this river comes me cranking in*
> *And cuts me from the best of all my land*
> *A huge half-moon, a monstrous cantle out...*

Surely he must have meant the Severn, but no:

> *I'll have this current in this place damm'd up;*
> *And here the smug and silver Trent shall run*
> *In a new channel, fair and evenly...*

24

Mortimer, perhaps, should have been the one to complain, but he was quite satisfied, possibly because he knew that, though his river did *come cranking in*, it seemed to leave the land all the better for it.

The Druids thought the behaviour of the river Severn was magic and no doubt the priests cashed in on it; they believed that the soul goes out Westwards with the sun and with the tide, to be stored in some mysterious islands in the West until such time as it must be born again. It can therefore be seen at once what a splendid natural analogy the Severn would offer. Mistletoe abounds everywhere in the Severn Estuary.

The approach to Upton-on-Severn is bad; the road goes across a hideous modern concrete bridge from which can be seen a picturesque group of houses above what was the barge-quay, and the tower of the old church has been left standing to enhance the scene.

Upton is a charming little Georgian town; Lloyd's Bank has original bow windows and there is a tailor and woollen draper whose shop must have offered the same appearance for at least one hundred and fifty years; it has a bow-window and well-worn step, and a fox's mask in the window to attract custom, presumably. Upon a stone-flagged alley is an entrancing tiny Baptist Chapel, dated 1734, with two kitten-like ears. Inside it is stark and varnished liberally with copal varnish, a bright brown, and is quite triumphantly itself.

Ripple next, a village with a sense of continuity and abiding peace. It stands at the very edge of the county boundary. It was a Roman settlement and here the Romans had a pottery. The church was the first in the diocese, being built at the junction of two old British trackways and it seems possible that proselytes from Kent, where the new religion was brought by the second St. Augustine, stopped at this quiet spot, calling it Ripple after the village in their own county, and founding the church about A.D. 680.

There are Saxon foundations which may not have been properly excavated before the present church was started because the present building leans oddly in all directions and looks as though it might topple over, like a child's house of cards. It won't, though. It has stood thus since 1190 or so and should last quite a bit longer even though it does not seem to have one straight wall or symmetrical arch. There is a very splendid complete set of misericords dating from the fifteenth century. They show the twelve monthly occupations of the villagers, that of July being the most interesting; it shows Lammas (Loaf-Mass) tide at the manorial bakery where disputes over weight and quality were usual; the village policeman, keeping order with a long truncheon appears by the oven door. These misericords look oddly out of place in the plain bare chancel and it is possible that at some time they were imported from elsewhere though the notes on the church do not say so.

In the churchyard is one of the giant's graves one comes across from time to time. They usually bear the same verse:

As you passe by, behold my length
But never glory in your strength.

25

The Ripple giant was Robert Reeve who died in 1626 aged fifty-six. It is said that he was 7 ft 4 in. high, the length of his body being the distance between head and foot stones, and it is also said that he died of a heart-attack mowing an acre of land for a bet. The cottages are grouped round a preaching cross and are so sentimentally pretty that the scene reminds one of the opening set for an old-fashioned pantomime: Jack and the Beanstalk with his mother and the bold bad baron must surely swagger out from one of the fairy-tale cottages.

The most south-westerly corner of the rough square of Shakespeare's country is Tewkesbury where, alas, yet another important battle must be recorded, but this one is of particular interest as it was conducted largely by a woman.

Queen Margaret, known as Margaret of Anjou, wife of Henry VI (who from time to time became insane), was afraid that her husband's malady would exclude her only son, Edward, Prince of Wales, from his claim to the throne. Aided by Warwick the Kingmaker, she arrived from France where she had been biding her time, landing at Weymouth in April 1471 to receive the bad news that the crown had been seized by the Yorkist Edward IV, who subsequently won a great battle at Barnet in which Warwick the Kingmaker was left dead on the field.

When the news reached Margaret she 'fell to the ground, her heart was pierced with sorrow and her spirits were tormented with melancholy', but two powerful Dukes who had escaped from Barnet assured her that the whole West of England was ready to rise in her support.

The new King Edward, hearing that the Queen was marching through the West Country, collecting levies, decided to put a stop to it and went westward with an army of Yorkists. He crossed the Cotswolds, came down through Painswick and stopped for refreshment at a village called Chiltenham. From there the army took the old track through Stoke Orchard to Tredington, where the King spent the night at the old Parsonage.

In the meantime the Queen, the Prince of Wales, and the Lancastrians were manoeuvring themselves into position at Tewkesbury, and next morning, Sunday May 4th, as the bells rang out from the abbey tower, the battle was joined in the fields between the Severn and the Avon, now known as *Bloody Meadow*.

The fate of the Prince of Wales has been immortalized by Shakespeare in the following scene, *Henry VI, (3)*, Act V, Scene V:

King Edward:	*Bring forth the gallant, let us hear him speak.*
	What! Can so young a thorn begin to prick?
	Edward, what satisfaction canst thou make
	For bearing arms, for stirring up my subjects.
	And all the troubles thou hast turned me to?

And the Prince replies haughtily:

> *Speak like a subject, proud, ambitious York!*
> *Suppose that I am now my father's mouth*

> *Resign thy chair, and where I stand kneel thou*
> *Whilst I propose the self-same words to thee,*
> *Which, traitor, thou would'st have me answer to.*
> *. . . . . .I tell ye all*
> *I am your better, traitors as ye are: –*
> *And thou usurp'st my father's right and mine.*

The Duke of Gloucester chips in with a nasty remark addressed to the Queen: 'That you might have still worn the petticoat, And ne'er have stol'n the breech from Lancaster.'

At which there ensues a frisky passage:

Queen Margaret: Ay, thou wast born to be a plague to men.

Gloucester: For God's sake take away this captive scold.

Prince Edward: Nay, take away this scolding crookback, rather.

The Prince appears not to have known when to come in out of the wet; he calls the King, Clarence and Gloucester respectively: lascivious Edward, perjured George, and misshapen Dick, at which all three stab him in the presence of his mother and other prisoners. The Duke of Gloucester subsequently became Richard III, and George, Duke of Clarence came to a sticky end in a butt of Malmsey wine (*sic*).

That description of the Prince's death demands a good deal of poet's licence; chroniclers of the day give the scene rather less gloriously, saying that Edward: 'was taken fleeinge to the townewards and slayne in the field.'

The common soldiers taken prisoner were freely pardoned, but the following Monday the Lancastrian leaders were court-martialled and beheaded at Tewkesbury Cross. Many other Lancastrians were slaughtered cruelly whilst taking refuge in various churches around, including the church at Didbrook, and many of the churches had to be re-dedicated on account of the blood shed within their walls.

Queen Margaret was broken-hearted, having nothing more to live for. She spent the next few days at the small priory at Deerhurst, near Tewkesbury. However, she recovered sufficiently to make a triumphant entry into London in the King's procession on May 21st, arriving in time to be with her husband when he died, two days later, in the Tower.

Tewkesbury Abbey is beyond praise; many people like it better than any of our great cathedrals; it has a wonderful atmosphere even though it is situated on the main Bristol-Birmingham road and transport lorries pass through continually.

It has a very grand Norman nave with great rounded pillars as solid as the pillars of Hercules and as you enter, instead of being oppressed by the great weight and strength of the masonry, you are immediately uplifted by the air of lightness; even on the darkest of November days, there is an almost honey-coloured glow in the church.

This must be due to the colour and texture of the marvellous stone of which it is built. Behind the High Altar is an ambulatory with a great deal of lacelike stone work, many fourteenth-century monuments and a number of small chapels.

After the battle the King went straight to the Abbey Church where he was escorted to the High Altar and 'gave unto Almighty God lawde and thanke for vyctorye that of His mercy He had that day graunted and gyven to him'.

With its splendid Romanesque Tower, the Abbey church stands with the mediaeval town clustering around and up to its gates. The town has some delightful timber-frame houses built in the old three-storied, overhanging style, a very fine old mill, and a great many alleys which are its own particular feature: Fish Alley, Mason's Court and so on.

The rivers here are wide and a pleasant afternoon can be spent hiring a boat and drifting through the peaceful green water-meadows which once were red with blood and where even now many skeletons of soldiers lie only a little way under the turf.

III The City of Worcester and Shakespeare's Villages

Two and a half miles from the City of Worcester, the London Road runs near the village of Whittington and on the left of the main road is a strange rounded hill, two hundred and eighty feet high, an ancient British earthwork, comparable to our pill-box strong points put up in concrete throughout the country at the beginning of the Second World War. Roman coins have been found there but no major excavations seem to have been made. At present, three trees grow on the summit and there is one curiously formed dead tree; it is a favourite spot for horses to stand on a summer's day and strongly resembles the man-made hills at Uppsala in Sweden where the great Vikings are buried, together with their wives and families, their households and their ships.

Worcester is Shakespeare's own city; the only metropolis he knew before he left Stratford-upon-Avon for London in his early twenties.

Having recovered from the irritation of the very considerable traffic jam at the bottlenecks where once were the gated entries to this ancient town, the visitor will discover one of the most interesting and exciting of all our cathedral cities.

Even those only midly interested in architecture will be fascinated by the rich diversity of the buildings; given a little time to wander round, one can find a sample of almost every period in architecture since the days of the Norman Conquest. The main street is a perfect demonstration of the fundamental unwillingness of the Englishman, in spite of all the present-day talk of townplanning, to plan a town. The streets retain their old names and shapes and the main street itself has examples of Queen Anne architecture at its best, in the Guildhall; half-timbered houses; samples of building under all the Georges; Edwardian baroque; Art Nouveau; Second Empire Renaissance; Scottish baronial; Regency; Gothic; Renaissance; Modernistic; Twentieth-Century Functional; and just under the cast-iron railway bridge which crosses over the road, squeezed in between it and a delightful Georgian coal merchants' office is a tiny blue and cream Moorish barber's.

Immediately opposite the charming group of almshouses called Berkeley's Hospital, with their quiet central cloister, is an overpowering bright red brick edifice, the Hop Market Commercial Hotel. A little further along is a large brick and terracotta Edwardian building strongly resembling Harrods. Few cities can boast of such a splendid number of Georgian houses: three-quarters of the main street is Georgian but the ground floors have been disguised with glass and chromium; banks have Georgian upper floors whilst the frontage is massive and important; the Golden Lion, opposite the Guildhall, is next to a Georgian building, the bottom half of which is a green glass and chromium shoe shop. Another pleasant half-timbered public house is standing waist-deep, as it were, in garish coloured tiles, a pseudo-Portuguese style.

Beyond the railway bridge, two modern cinemas glare at each other across the road, and further along is a row of good houses of the Georgian period. W. H. Smith & Son have left their building almost untouched and the house where Sir Charles Hastings, founder of the British Medical Association lived, 1794–1866, has a splendid upper part.

The old church of St. Martin's, which has an original three-tiered pulpit, is down a side street; immediately in front of the gate, and within two yards of its railing, is a public convenience set at such an angle that you have to skirt it in order to enter the church. Crowded against this church is a school, originally endowed by Queen Elizabeth the First and rebuilt in 1735, and immediately beyond it are black-and-white timbered buildings, leaning delightfully forward as though they would rest against the church walls out of sheer weariness of old age. Beyond this is the Cornmarket, a wide-open space which in Shakespeare's time must have been surrounded with old balconied black-and-white houses, a good sample of which still exists, carefully preserved, a stone's-throw away.

In the corner of this old market place is a tiny house called *Ye olde King Charles House* where Charles lodged before the battle of Worcester and from which it is said he escaped by the back door when the Cromwellian soldiers entered by the front. This must have entailed considerable agility as the back seems to be built up and surrounded by incredibly old buildings. The house seems remarkably small to have sheltered so important a paying guest; the main bedroom, overlooking the market place, has a sliding window and over the door is the inscription:

LOVE GOD   W. BIS77RD   HONOR $\overline{Y}^{e}$ KINGE.

It has a serpentine-fronted window and next door there is a corn-merchant's with two delightful bow-fronted windows.

The City of Worcester Dental Clinic is housed in an interesting Georgian Gothic building of considerable charm, with a small garden in front.

Mrs Henry Wood, the Victorian best-selling writer, whose novels include *The Channings, Mrs Halliburton's Troubles* and, best known, *East Lynne*, was born and lived in Worcester until she was twenty-one. Some of her writing is almost documentary and gives a vivid picture of middle and lower-class life in Worcester in the eighteen forties and fifties. For instance, the Great Western Railway line, from London to Birmingham, did not touch Worcester until later; passengers to that city were obliged to get out at Birmingham and take a long journey into Worcester by stage coach. In *Mrs Halliburton's Troubles* she describes how, when the family moved to Worcester, young Mrs Halliburton and her small daughter travelled from Birmingham inside the stage coach but that Mr Halliburton and their three sons travelled on top, outside the crowded coach. There was a severe storm and Mr. Halliburton was soaked through, getting an attack of rheumatic fever from which he never recovered. He died slowly, in the way which writers of that period so much enjoyed describing, and young Mrs Halliburton toiled at glove-making in order to keep herself, her young family and the maid-servant. The house in which they all lived is described as being a small one on the London road with a glorious view from the back windows across to the Malvern Hills. There are still a number of houses which answer this description and it is fun trying to decide which one was Mrs Halliburton's.

The Cathedral of St. Mary is built upon high ground above the Severn, which sometimes is in flood almost to the Cathedral walls. The river is seen to great advantage from the Cathedral grounds, running wide and slow, and on the opposite bank are the low-lying green playing fields upon which the great battle of Worcester was fought in 1651 between the young King Charles Stuart and General Oliver Cromwell and their armies, and at which the King was finally defeated and fled on his historic journey of escape into France.

The battle was watched by the King from the tower of the Cathedral until such time as he descended himself into the fray to drive Cromwell back across the river. But on those flat fields six thousand of his men were killed or taken prisoner and the history books say that the battle continued till nightfall, so September 3rd must have been a pretty crowded day.

Worcester City itself was solidly Royalist, so much so that it is said in the history of Gloucester that, shortly after the Restoration of Charles II, the King, bitterly remembering his father's defeat before that City, ordered the gates to be pulled down and presented them to the City of Worcester, which had long remained faithful to his cause.

Worcester likes to be known as The Faithful City. The very fine Guildhall, built in 1727 by a pupil of Wren, has over the doorway the Latin inscription: *May the Faithful City Flourish.* On either side of the door are statues of Carolus I and Carolus II, strangely foreshortened, and over the centre of the door is the head of what looks like the devil, nailed by his large ears. It is difficult for us now to realise just how strongly feelings in the Civil War did run, but this is said to represent the head of Cromwell and is a sly dig at the Commonwealth by the architect whose ancestors must have been strongly in the resistance movement.

It is interesting to read what one of the Commonwealth generals, Nehemiah Wharton, wrote about Worcester:

> *Worcestershire is a pleasant, fruitful and rich country, abounding with corn, woods, pasture, hills, and valleys, every hedge and highway beset with fruit, but especially with pears, whereof they make that pleasant drink called perry, which they sell for a penny a quart, though better than ever you tasted in London. The city is more large than any I have seen since I left London; it abounds in outward things, but for the want of the Word the people perish. It is pleasantly seated, exceedingly populous and doubtless very rich, on the east bank of the famous river Severn, the walls in a form of a triangle and the gates seven. There is a very stately cathedral called St Mary's in which there are many stately monuments; amongst the rest, in the middle of the quire is the monument of King John, all of white marble, with his picture thereon to the life. Sir, our army did little think ever to have seen Worcester, but the Providence of God hath brought us thither and had it not, the city is so vile, resembles Sodom, and is the very emblem of Gomorrah, and doubtless it would have been worse than either Algiers or Malta – a very den of thieves, and a receptacle and refuge for all the hell-hounds of the country.*

He had worse things to say about Hereford!
An historian of Worcester, writing in 1856, says:

Royal Oak Day, May 29th, is wonderfully shorn of its honours since people have generally taken to read history, and have learned how little reason they have to bless the memory of the Stuarts. The marvellous escape of Charles II when his pursuers passed under the oak tree in which he was secreted after the battle of Worcester, is now only commemorated in the city which boasts of being 'faithful' to its kings whether their memory be odorous or not, by some half-dozen boughs of oak being affixed over as many doorways in different streets.

Thus does the pendulum swing from century to century. A certain sober and righteous Brigadier in a Scottish regiment was seen recently, on being suddenly confronted with a marble bust of King Charles I, to snatch off his hat.

If a faithful city, it is also a very thriving industrial centre with factories and engineering works of all kinds. Amongst the products are carpets, vinegar (the famous Worcester Sauce), gloves and china. The enemy considered it a profitable target during the Second World War and it was badly bombed, particularly the area near the Cathedral; beside the river, many warehouses, shops and small industries have been completely demolished. This has been cleared, leaving a large empty space, now used as a Car Park, from the centre of which the graceful spire, which is all that is left of St. Andrew's rises very effectively.

The oldest industries are glove manufacture and the making of fine porcelain. The two names connected with glove-making are Dent and Fownes, the latter founding the industry in 1777, both these names being used today in the trade.

Mrs Henry Wood describes the streets of Worcester in the mid-nineteenth century as being alive with glove-operatives. There were parers, grounders, leather-sorters, dyers, cutters, makers-up, and so on: 'all being necessary, besides the sewing, to turn out one pair of gloves.' The wages varied according to the work, ability and the man's industry, from fifteen shillings to twenty-five shillings per week. If a man gained more than twenty-five, he had a stated salary, as was the case with the foremen. These wages, Mrs Henry Wood says, joined to what was earned by the women, were sufficient to maintain a comfortable home and to bring up children decently.

The women operatives were called gloveresses; they would work in their own houses 'whilst rocking the cradle with one foot'. Some made the gloves; that is, seamed the fingers together and put in the thumbs; these were called *makers*. The *welters* hemmed the gloves round the edge of the wrist. Those who worked the ornamental lines across the back were called *pointers*. Some of the work was done by a patent machine whereby the stitches were perfectly equal, the author states naively, and she goes on to say that 'some of the stouter gloves were stitched together instead of being sewn; stitching so beautifully regular and neat that a stranger would look at it in admiration'.

The manufacturing process has altered very little in the past two centuries; in spite of all the recent machinery invented a great deal of glove-making is still done by hand, in private houses, as in Shakespeare's day.

Shakespeare refers no less than forty-nine times to gloves:

Oh, that I were a glove upon that hand
That I might touch that cheek!

He refers to 'the glover's paring knife' and almost certainly he was quite familiar with the industry from his visits to the city.

About Worcester procelain whole books have been written. The Royal Worcester Porcelain factory extends a welcome to any visitors, who are escorted round their modern factory and shown all the fascinating processes by which they produce their world-famous china.

But it is impossible to mention Worcester china without remembering the lively and exciting personage of Dr John Wall, who first put Worcester china on the map. Original specimens of Dr Wall china now fetch fabulous prices in the sale rooms but, in his day, Dr John Wall was more noted as a physician and research chemist; his love of colours turned him to painting as a hobby. He was possessed with a burning energy, a lively mind and tremendous initiative.

Born at Powick in 1708, the son of a tradesman of Worcester, he attended the King's School and was later elected scholar of Worcester College, Oxford, and finally took a degree in medicine at St. Thomas's Hospital and set up as a doctor in Foregate Street, Worcester, where he gained a great reputation as a practical physician. One of his hobby horses was Malvern Waters for which he made many exaggerated claims.

As far as we are concerned in the present day, the experiments in colour which he undertook with several friends in his laboratory, the introduction of fine new colours inspired by oriental china, and the application of new methods of applying these colours to the porcelain then being made in Worcester, is by far the most important thing Dr Wall did.

In later life he found painting a relaxation and painted a great many large epic scenes which were greatly admired. A biography printed in 1820 says that the great Lord Lyttelton asserts 'that if he had not been one of the first physicians, he would have been one of the first painters of the age'. It goes on to say:

His guardian, Lord Sandys, apprehensive that the smell of oil colours would injure his health, or that it might otherwise suffer from this sedentary amusement, when added to the more necessary pursuit of his literary studies, deprived him of the means of prosecuting his favourite pursuit. To obviate the deprivation of colours, he, it is said, has frequently saved the juice of his currant pudding, and with it tinted his juvenile attempts.

Which goes to show how fussy about their health they were in those days, though it is possible that Dr Wall was allergic to the smell of oil paint.

The biography goes on, in rather a carelessly-written passage:

His oil paintings in later life were the source of attraction to every stranger visiting Worcester; among others, Garrick, whose quick and vivacious manner of jumping upon the chairs to assist this great little actor in his nearer approach to the pictures, is still known by tradition in this city.

His better-known pictures have rather fearsome titles: *The Head of Pompey brought to Caesar* was bought by Lord Lyttelton for Hagley, *Moses striking the Rock, Elijah fed by the Ravens* and *The Shunamite's Child Restored* give us some idea of the kind of thing he painted.

He was a sufferer from gout:

> *Such was his dislike to make those uneasy around him that, during those fits of the gout to which he was a martyr, he insisted on being attended only by his man servant, lest, in the agony of pain he should cause those he loved, and would otherwise be about him, to suffer with him.*

Alas, the Malvern Waters, for which he was such an enthusiastic advocate, did not, apparently, help his gout. He went to Bath for treatment; there he died and is buried in the Abbey Church with a splendidly eulogistic memorial which ends:

> *Husbands, Fathers, Friends and Neighbours*
> *saw in him*
> *a living pattern of their duties*
> *and must ever remember*
> *the various excellencies of that Heart*
> *the loss of which they now lament.*
>
> *
>
> *He died June 27, 1776*
> *Aged 67*

That was no doubt true, but what is certain is that the living patterns of his art still delight those proud possessors of an original piece of *Dr Wall china*.

And now to the highly controversial matter of Shakespeare's marriage licence, a subject which makes scholars pale and students of Shakespeare tremble with passion.

It must be true that the man within whom genius was to ripen into a blaze of glory was, in his childhood and youth, entirely unremarkable. One of eight children of a jolly, ordinary townsman of Stratford-upon-Avon, he went to school there, grew up, married at eighteen and, some years later, left the town and his wife and three children without attracting any attention whatever. Everything we know about him, and it is very little, has had to be dredged up from old parish registers, or else hangs upon legend or conjecture. We assume that he must have done certain things in and around Stratford because they were what any other young townsman of his time would do. The issue is considerably confused by the name Shakespeare being a common one, and the spelling of the time being treated light-heartedly in the extreme, as we see in the case of Celia Fiennes.

The undoubted fact is that, in the episcopal register at Worcester, there is an entry dated November 27th, 1582, noting the issue of a marriage licence to *William Shaxpere* and Anne Whateley of Temple Grafton. In the same place on November

28th of the same year, the very next day, two yeomen of Stratford, Fulk Sandells and John Richardson, agreed to pay forty pounds if the marriage of *William Shagspere* and *Anne Hathaway* of Stratford in the Diocese of Worcester, maiden, did not take place.

Thereby could hang a very splendid tale indeed; the future Bard, a young man of eighteen, getting himself tangled up with Anne Hathaway, a maiden of twenty-six when he was really in love with someone called Anne Whateley of Temple Grafton; the young man wilfully rushing to Worcester for a licence to marry Whateley followed hot-foot by two indignant yeoman-friends of Hathaway, determined to see justice done to the young woman already three months gone with child.

But looking at it in the cold light of reason, it must all be a matter of spelling. What is known as Anne Hathaway's cottage at Shottery was not, in fact, her cottage at all, but that of her step-mother, Joan Hathaway where, after her father's death, Anne stayed with her three stepbrothers. It is perfectly possible that she did not get on very well with her step-mother, or even that her step-mother, having discovered that she was pregnant, turned her out of the house, so that she found shelter at Temple Grafton, a village a mile or two away. The bond may well be money payable as an indemnity on account of young Shakespeare being a minor.

The mind pictures a charming, modest little Anne Whateley versus an older, plainer, rather desperate Anne Hathaway for the honour of whom two yeoman of Stratford were prepared to pay forty pounds (which was a lot of money in those days), but it is, alas, only too probable that they were one person.

There is no existing record of Shakespeare's marriage to Anne Hathaway. Luddington Church, three miles from Stratford, has been mentioned, as have Temple Grafton Church and also St. Martin's Church, Worcester, but, in the case of St. Martin's, two pages have been removed from the parish register which contained the relevant dates; therefore nothing can be proved. Anyone with a large house of suitable situation and age, with the remains of a small room which may once have been the private chapel of the household, can claim that Shakespeare and Anne Hathaway were married there and no one can prove that they were not.

Over the years, keen Shakespearean scholars have scoured the villages round Stratford, carefully scrutinized parish registers, dug into innumerable civic records, probed county manuscripts, investigated legends and traditions and inquired into old customs but, so far, no one has made any discovery which has shed any real light upon the young man William Shakespeare.

There is an ancient rhyme, attributed without foundation to Shakespeare and too paltry to repeat, which mentions, with an adjective for each, eight villages, now loosely referred to as Shakespeare's villages. They are Pebworth, Long Marston, Hillborough, Temple Grafton, Exhall, Wixford, Broom and Bidford.

Bidford is the largest of these, a small town on the road which Shakespeare would probably take quite frequently from Stratford to Evesham Market. It is of Roman origin, being situated on Rycknield Street and has a Roman ford through the river which could easily be negotiated by somebody with the know-how. A very delightful bridge was built over the Avon to replace the ford by the monks of Alcester.

Built of grey stone, it has alcoves into which the pedestrian can step to avoid passing traffic; in any of these, Shakespeare must often have leaned to look over into the quietly flowing water below.

Long Marston possesses *King's Lodge* where Charles II spent the night as a fugitive when he was disguised as Jane Lane's servant on his escape from Worcester. In later years His Majesty told the story of his escape personally to Pepys. The incident at Long Marston is of the same genre as the story told of King Alfred and the burnt cakes, but must be more authentic. It is said that the King, disguised as Miss Lane's personal servant Will Jackson, was in the kitchen whilst the meal was being prepared, and probably getting under the feet of the busy cook who told him to make himself useful winding up the Jack. He made a complete botch of it and the angry cook cried: 'What county man are you that you know not how to wind up a Jack?' and the King replied suavely: 'I am a poor tenant's son of Colonel Lane in Staffordshire. We seldom have roast meat, but when we have we don't make use of the Jack.' The answer evidently satisfied the cook as the next day the party proceeded to Chipping Campden and thence to Cirencester. At the Restoration, Jane Lane was granted an annuity of a thousand pounds in recognition of her services.

Hillsborough, off the Evesham-Stratford road, is hardly a village at all, though at one time possession of it was shared by some important people including one of the de Montforts.

Billsley, slightly to the north, on the Stratford-Alcester road, is another of the places where Shakespeare is said to have been married but the only known fact is that his grand-daughter, Elizabeth Hall, was married there to John Barnard, who was later knighted. The manor house has an Elizabethan wing with panelling said to have been brought from New Place, the Halls' house in Stratford, and there is a room referred to as *Shakespeare's Room*, where he is supposed to have slept when he visited his grand-daughter.

In nearly all the local history books there is quite considerable mention of Salford Hall, the manor house at Abbot's Salford, with many illustrations in both line and colour. This house is fifty yards or so from the main Evesham-Stratford road and must have been passed many a time by Shakespeare, if not actually visited. It is approached by a straight drive, through a black-and-white gatehouse with a pointed gable immediately over the entrance, now used as a barn, which frames a delightful approach to a charming house, now unoccupied except for people waiting for other accommodation living temporarily in the later additions at the back.

This house is a really superb example of an Elizabethan stone-built mansion built in 1602, though the date over the door is given erroneously as 1662. It contains three of the best priest's hiding holes in existence, some beautiful old glass, marvellously proportioned rooms and a great long gallery at the top of the house up and down which the ladies of the day would promenade for their exercise in weather which was too bad to allow them to walk anywhere outside. But, alas, it is practically a ruin. Standing quietly for a few minutes you can actually hear bits of plaster falling, like slow tears. The stairs are no longer safe; many of the windows, some of them containing the old Elizabethan greenish glass, are broken and the whole edifice is in a shocking state of disrepair.

Sir William Dugdale, the great historian, who lived in Shakespeare's time and who wrote the first full authentic history of Warwickshire, has much to say about the house. He claims that the name is derived from a salt spring found in the near neighbourhood. The first house was built upon the site in the twelfth century and belonged to the Abbey of Evesham. The second house was built by monks and was half-timbered. And what in Dugdale's time (1602) was the new house was erected and occupied by the family of Alderford. At one time it was owned by the very ancient family of Eyston whose arms are three golden lions rampant. It was through the Eystons that the Lord Chancellor, Sir Thomas More, afterwards canonised by the Catholic Church, lived here for a time with his wife and family.

The house has always had strong Catholic connections and for thirty years or so was occupied by a community of Benedictine nuns from Cambrai who took refuge there from the French Revolution.

Looking through the back windows, one can see that a bewildering amount of additions and repairs have been made from time to time but, if something is not done quickly, the house will be beyond repair. Houses show so definitely and rapidly when they are no longer loved and cared for; they need people living in them and Salford is simply crying out for attention.

Deviating only slightly from the road to Worcester from Stratford brings one into the country of the Lenches and the Bevingtons, Wood and Cock Bevington, both of which are in the parish of Salford. As one usually finds, the two hamlets were the property of the church, in this case Evesham Abbey, and after the Dissolution were given to private owners. The property of Wood Bevington was sold by the Randolphs to St. John's College, Oxford, who leased it to Mr Secretary Conway, whose descendants occupied it for three hundred years on condition that representatives of the college were to be entertained at the manor whenever they made a tour of inspection. In those days, these hamlets were very isolated and, whenever they left home, the family were accompanied by mounties armed to the teeth with pistols. The present manor house is a delightful red-brick building with white-painted latticed windows in charming surroundings.

The terrain is slightly unfamiliar and gives an almost Provençal impression at a casual glance owing to the regular planting of fruit trees, the old-established apple trees looking vaguely like olive and cork trees and the young newly-planted orchards resembling vineyards.

Lench is the old English word for small hill and there are a number of Lenches: Atch, Church, Hob, Rous and Sherriffs Lench.

Rous Lench is a strange little triangular village, its tiny church having no tower. The church school is a find for anyone keen on Victoriana; it has a very steep gabled roof with bright chocolate brown scalloped bargeboards and is laden with encaustic tiling and everything to delight the heart of anyone who is Betjeman-minded.

The church itself is a little weird, having been strangely restored with a distinct Moorish, or even Saracen flavour and retaining its hanging Victorian oil lamps which would be the envy of a certain new and smart little London restaurant with Victorian décor. Red glass, frosted glass and delightfully patterned, they hang incongruously amongst the Norman arches and fragments of Saxon stonework. There is a set of Jacobean black and gilded chairs in the chancel said to be extremely valuable and the processional cross is believed to have been used at the coronation of one of the Tudor monarchs and is made of solid gold. There is a memorial to Edward Rous dated 1611, showing one son and three daughters, and another memorial to Elizabeth Lady Rous, his daughter-in-law, with one of those long amusing eulogies which make one feel sadly lacking in virtues:

...much of her soul had heretofore
accompanied the mournfull obesequies unto
the same cold manstion below which returning
weakend with greife for so great alose she,
awhile after became dispirited by adead palsy,
that so she affected to live and die. –
Nevertheless there was vigour enough left in
her tongue – lived and dyed 12 March anno 169½

Outside, over the Norman doorway, is an extremely rare small carving set in the wall, representing Our Lord.

Lench Court, standing on the hillside above the church, was once a Cromwellian stronghold. The part bordering the road is genuine Tudor timbered building of the best and rarest kind. It was one side of a square manor house with a courtyard in the centre, entered by the large archway still to be seen and surrounded by a moat. All but the remaining quarter has disappeared to make way for rebuilding in the black-and-white manner; but it is grand in a way that Tudor building never was, the whole forming an L round a delightful forecourt leading to the gardens of seven acres built up the hillside in terraces. Here are to be seen the most magnificent examples of topiary in the county; a marquee in yew, and what represents a row of cottages and other very fine specimens. A small company of gardeners has to be established on scaffolding for the yearly clipping of these marvellous hedges. The garden mounts in flights of stone steps to a folly tower from which can be seen a magnificent view of the surrounding countryside.

Cromwell often used to walk in this garden and one of the Rous family, a strong Cromwellian, was taken prisoner by the Royalists in his own garden and clapped into Warwick Castle, where he died; his body was later returned to his home and buried in the church.

As with the church, there is about the garden a strange alien flavour. It is far from typical; for instance, there is a magnificent cedar tree and a few yards away a fine specimen of monkey puzzle.

A little further towards Alcester is Inkberrow, a much larger village than Rous Lench, through which, almost certainly, Shakespeare often went on his way to Worcester. And what thirsty traveller would not call at The Bull? This tiny delightful inn must look exactly as it did three hundred years ago. Inkberrow was strongly Royalist; the King and his armies stayed there on Sunday, May 11th, 1645, and the King accidently left behind his book of maps in the front of which is the inscription:

The Kingdome of England and Principality
of Wales exactly described with every sheere
and the small townes in every one of them,
on six mappes portable for every man's pocket;
useful for all commanders for quarteringe
of souldiers, and all sorts of persons that
would be informed where the armies be – never
so commodiously drawne before this 1644.
Described by one that travailed throughout
the whole Kingdome for its purpose.

An interesting example of seventeenth-century publisher's blurb!

IV Great Houses near Stratford

Within a few miles of Stratford-upon-Avon are three great houses, Charlecote, Ettington Park and Compton Verney, all within walking distance of that town. Charlecote is the best-known of these, perhaps, because of the legend about Shakespeare and the deer. But there is no proof that he was associated with Charlecote any more than with the others. Compton Verney and Ettington also had deer parks and, though the deer have gone, the parks still remain. All three houses have been rebuilt since Shakespeare's day, and all were in the possession of one or other of the great old families of England.

Charlecote belongs, as it has since Shakespeare's day, to the Fairfax-Lucys; the turreted gate-house, which is part of the original building, is the property of the National Trust and the house is thrown open to visitors.

The Avon is very much a stripling above Stratford, weedy and unimportant-looking in some places; it might be any stream, but we know it is the Avon and therefore glamorous. At Charlecote the thrill is to see the great stag, with his huge ungainly antlers, standing in the rushes drinking from the Avon.

Ettington Park and Compton Verney; two houses. But how different! One seems to shout: 'Look at me! I'm a very important house indeed, built by Top People for Top People.' And the other stands in silent dignity, saying nothing at all but being a very important house built by Top People for Top People.

Ettington Park, the property of the Underhills and later the Earldom of Ferrers, is now an hotel. The alterations to the house, completed in 1862, were described by the then owner as being in the 'advanced early English style'. But the ordinary un-instructed observer today might describe it as 'by Scottish baronial hall out of French Château-of-the-Loire', with a whole lot of oddments stuck on regardless. The front entrance lurches forward clumsily into the drive with a kind of Gothic ambulatory on either side, roofless and draughty. Scenes from the lives of the previous owners are carved below the bay windows and, like cherries on a birthday cake, coloured shields of armorial bearings are scattered about here and there.

In the garden are two large greenhouses separated by a square stone-built porch surmounted by stone pine-apples at each of its four corners. In this is a family coach with the arms of the family emblazoned on the side.

The garden and the surroundings are delightful and, in a beautiful setting within a few yeards of the house, is Ettington Old Church of which the tower and part of the south transept still remain. Trees have grown round these ruins in a particularly felicitous way. Nobody seems to know why what was once the parish church should have fallen into ruins; the historian Dugdale noted that it was the only parish in Warwickshire which had so long and uninterrupted a succession of owners who could trace their line back to the days before the Norman Conquest.

The roof of the bell tower in the old church is a series of small, beautifully carved oak panels and there are two splendid brasses of Underhills, now fixed to the wall. On a white board are some verses taken from the tomb of one Anthony Underhill; the last verse reads:

As dreams doe slyde as bubbles rise and fall
As flowers doe fade and flourish in an hower
As smoke doth rise and vapours vanish all
Beyond the witt or reach of human power
As somers heat doth parch the withered grass
Such is or stay so lyfe of man doth passe,

Anthony Underhill died the XVI day of July
Anno DNI 1587

Though not brilliant the verses are a long way above the average tombstone poetry. Scholars are extremely sceptical when Shakespeare's name is mentioned in connection with these verses. But they *could be* by Shakespeare. His twins, Hamnet and Judith, were baptised at Stratford on February 2nd, 1585, and at the time the verses were written he would be a young man of twenty-three. When looking round for a rhymer to write verses for the dear departed, the Underhills might quite well have heard of a young man in Stratford who had a certain ability and have invited him to write a few verses for them. Whatever anyone may think of the quality of the poetry, it does reflect the way the brain of Shakespeare worked at times:

As smoke doth rise and vapours vanish all
Beyond the will or reach of human power –

Surely, surely, we know the mind behind these thoughts?

The country south-east to north-east of Stratford-upon-Avon, from Shipston-on-Stour up to Warwick and Kenilworth, is wonderfully rich and quite different from the rest of the area we call 'Shakespeare's Country'. There are oak trees in better fettle than those in Windsor Great Park; the whole terrain looks as though it had been set out as a park with gigantic trees standing knee deep, in July, in fields of golden corn. The Fosse Way rips through, straight as an arrow, from Moreton-in-Marsh, along the Vale of the Red Horse, below Edgehill, and on into Northamptonshire and the Fen Country. Just South of Wellesbourne and bordering the Fosse Way is Compton Verney park with its two lakes.

Compton Verney is so gorgeous that it is going to be difficult not to stun the reader with over-praise, as do the church memorials describing people in line after line of nothing but virtues. The first sight of the house, standing on beautifully-kept lawns, surrounded by a deliberately planned tree-background, with a strategically placed bridge dividing two lily-grown lakes, is breathtaking. When you learn that the house was built by Adam and the garden planned by Lancelot Brown, you may think that this combination of the brains of men of genius has never produced anything better.

The historian Dugdale was a great friend of the Verneys and put a lot of work into research into the family history. He gave the family a first edition of his book. He describes the earlier house as 'the splendid old house near the Poole' with the 'Houses

41

of the Towne' to the east. There is no town left now and as far as one can see there is a park of splendid oaks.

Vanbrugh, who designed Blenheim Palace, is supposed to have had a hand in the building of the house. About his architectural ability, a contemporary wit suggested his epitaph should read:

Lie heavy on him earth for he
Laid many heavy loads on thee!

But the period demanded heavy and ponderous building and all the greater credit lies with Vanbrugh and Adam that in re-building Compton Verney they created a massive house which does not give the appearance of heaviness.

According to Dugdale the property was at one time owned by Alice Ferrers, the famous and ambitious mistress of Edward III, grandfather of the 'little princes in the Tower' who, it is said, was a good king until his declining years when he became completely under her influence. As an example of her rapacity, it is said of her that she took a ring she wanted from the finger of the king as he lay on his death-bed. She was impeached, which means she got a thorough censuring from the House of Lords, backed up by the House of Commons, but she seems to have got over it all right because she married Sir William Windsor and had a daughter through whom the house passed to the Verneys. In the days in which Dudgale wrote, it was called Compton Murdak after the family who owned the manor. The plain Georgian chapel contains splendid effigies and glass which tell the family history of the Verneys.

Though there is a caretaker and gardener, the house has stood empty for a great many years, and is still empty, but recently the whole estate, including the acres of parkland, has been sold and not for private habitation. The heart jumps nervously at the sight of several great oaks lying felled, like fallen warriors, and one hopes that nothing worse is going to happen.

Through Wellesbourne to Warwick, and, entering Warwick, one gets a glimpse of the castle reflected in the river. This is probably England's most perfect existing mediaeval castle with the mediaeval town clustering round it. Celia Fiennes says:

...the towne of Warwick by means of a sad fire about 4 or 5 year since (1694) that laid the greatest part in ashes, its most now new buildings which is brick and coyn'd with stone and the windows the same; there still remains some few houses of the old town which are all built of stone; the streetes are very handsome and the building regular and fine, not very lofty being limited by act of parliament to such a pitch and size to build the town; the ruines of the Church still remaines the repairing of which is the nexte worke design'd.

In Warwick it is easy to see how mediaeval towns were completely closed in by their walls and gateways. The east and west gateways still exist, forming traffic bottlenecks, and traces of the old ramparts are to be seen on either side of the gates. The town provides days of happy exploration to the student of history; there can be few towns left in Europe upon which the hand of 'progress' has descended more lightly.

Between Warwick and Kenilworth, to the right of the road, lies the house called Guy's Cliff. The present house is of no particular virtue and is falling into ruins; the estate has been sold and for some time was used as a dirt track for motor-cycle racing. Houses are now appearing almost overnight but the actual land upon which all this is taking place is steeped in history. Guy of Warwick was an exciting legend long before Shakespeare was born; at the back of the house there is a surprisingly sudden cliff rising from the river in which are caves and an underground passage which may have been connected at one time with Warwick Castle. In these caves Guy of Warwick is said to have lived as a hermit for many years, and all for love.

Almost next door is the old Saxon Mill, now an expensive restaurant, but well worth a visit, if you can afford it. It is built over the Avon, which froths out from the mill race into a wide-spreading stretch of water flanked by Guy's Cliff. The old mill house has been attractively done up in the simple gingham tablecloth style; the downstairs bar has a paving stone of the floor replaced by a slab of glass beneath which the Avon can be seen rushing purposefully through, a yard or so beneath one's feet and for the amazement of visitors the old mill wheel, well oiled, is to be seen slowly turning. There are tables and chairs set out in front at which you can sit having drinks and looking out over the foam, which may be mostly detergent, and enjoying the really delightful scene.

Fortified by this interlude you will be able to tackle Stoneleigh Abbey, a mile or so off the road to Kenilworth. The Avon here is disappointingly scruffy; the present Stoneleigh Abbey is a very splendid house indeed and should be situated on a grand expanse of water, instead of which the rushes grow and the ducks quack round in the mud, paying no more respect than they would pay to the village pond.

The old Abbey, as can be seen from the delightful gatehouse, was built of blocks of that wonderful reddish Warwickshire stone, warm and soft.

Dugdale says that the original Abbey was founded by Queen Matilda for the Cistercian Order. Once again we hear that at the Dissolution the buildings and land were handed to private ownership, in this case to the Leighs, who have held it since then and still live there. The new house was built, incorporating part of the old abbey, in 1720 and contains some splendid pictures of the family by Van Dyck, Lely and Kneller. One Chandos Leigh was at Harrow with Lord Byron, who became his great friend and of whom there are two fine portraits. Chandos himself seems to have been very much the same type of good-looking young-man-about-town as Byron, he is shown lounging gracefully, if arrogantly, with an abundance of carelessly arranged curly hair and large candid eyes.

The first Lord Leigh entertained Charles I here when he had a cold reception at Coventry. But this Royal visit is much overshadowed by the full-dress visit of Queen Victoria with the Prince Consort in 1858 when the Queen waved to the cheering multitude from a balcony. The Royal visitors only stayed two nights but the preparations made to receive them were prodigious; some of the old original Chippendale furniture, chairs and tables and serpentine chests, were enamelled white and gold,

43

rooms were re-papered, a special bedspread was made and hand-embroidered, new china was ordered and emblazoned with the unicorn's head (part of the Leigh coat-of-arms), new carpets were laid, and even a pin-cushion beautifully embroidered with V.R. was placed on the frilled dressingtable to be used by the Queen. Gifts were exchanged and a good time said to be had by all.

Jane Austen was a relative of the Leighs but, though a great lover of visits to other people's houses, she did not stay at Stoneleigh until she was thirty, by which time she had written *Northanger Abbey* and sold it to a publisher who put it into cold storage for thirteen years. (In the introduction the author says: 'That any bookseller should think it worth while to purchase what he did not think it worth while to publish seems extra-ordinary.') But what is even more extraordinary is that Northanger Abbey so strongly resembles Stoneleigh that Jane Austen herself was amazed and attributes the resemblance to dreams.

> *They returned to the hall, that the chief stair-case might be ascended, and the beauty of its wood, and ornaments of rich carving might be pointed out: having gained the top, they turned in an opposite direction from the gallery in which her room lay, and shortly entered one of the same plan, but superior in length and breadth. She was here shewn successively into three large bed-chambers, with their dressing-rooms, most completely and handsomely fitted up; everything that money and taste could do, to give comfort and elegance to apartments, had been bestowed on these; and, being furnished within the last five years, they were perfect in all that would be generally pleasing, and wanting in all that could give pleasure to Catherine.*

Two rivers run through the luxurious parkland of Stoneleigh; below the house the Avon is joined by the river Sowe and the road runs over the splendid mediaeval Stare bridge built by the monks. It seems unbelievable that all this rich, glorious country should be within so short a distance of the industrial heart of England, the Black Country.

Stoneleigh village itself is extremely attractive and was at one time strategically important as being at the junction of several roads; the roads from Warwick to Coventry and from Southam to Birmingham cross here but the village has retained an atmosphere of peace and quiet and is quite charming. It, too, has a very fine more modern bridge over the quietly-flowing river Sowe, shaded by trees. The village is built mostly in red sandstone, the almshouses dated 1594 being a very perfect example of their kind. In the exact centre of the village, on the rising ground of the village green, is a brick-built Victorian forge, dated 1851, with an upsidedown horse-shoe in different-coloured brick on the main wall. There are many ancient brick and timber cottages, some of them built in the very old cruck-hung style with tie-beams.

The church is famous for the Norman doorway and chancel arch, and is built in the same red sandstone. The box pews are fitted with brass candlesticks. There is a great tomb to the only English woman ever created a duchess in her own right; Alice, daughter of Sir Thomas Leigh and wife of the famous Robert Dudley, Earl of Leicester, whose relations with Elizabeth the Great are still the subject of controversy, and whose first wife, Amy Robsart, was found dead in very suspicious circumstances. Alice Dudley lived to be ninety; her daughter, who lies in a tier below, having died forty-eight years before.

And now to Kenilworth and to the most splendid party ever given. At the present time Kenilworth looks more like a ruined factory than one of the glorious castles of England and a yard-by-yard description of it would merely be describing what *was* rather than what *is*. It was, however, a very important place indeed and is strongly knit up in the history of England.

Long before Shakespeare's day, the land was thickly forested and the roads running from town to town were infested by robbers and highwaymen. In order that travellers should have time to prepare themselves for attack, the Constable of Warwickshire ordered that the roadway should be cleared on either side to the width of six acres. At one time the castle belonged to John of Gaunt who, with his three wives, was the progenitor of so many Kings and Queens; and it was whilst he was staying here, with his mistress Catherine Swynford, whom he married late in life, that he heard that his palace of the Savoy in the Strand, London, had been burned to the ground in the Peasant's Revolt.

Queen Elizabeth gave the castle to Robert Dudley, Earl of Leicester, and he received her here four times in 1566, 1568 (when Shakespeare was four), 1572 and 1575. In this last year, Leicester was particularly anxious to please the Queen; he and Elizabeth were now both forty-two and he had contracted a secret marriage to Lady Sheffield which he was not too happy about. He accordingly planned an entertainment for his Sovereign which was to wipe away all hard feelings. The Queen, to the very great benefit of the country, was economical to the point of meanness, but she very much enjoyed having money spent upon her own entertainment and this Robert Dudley did on such a big scale that it was as though Kenilworth went up in a blaze of expenditure, never to regain its glory. This party to end all parties lasted for eighteen days of July at the end of one of the Queen's summer progresses. The Earl had recently added a wing to the castle with fine mullioned windows, in the latest style, and furnished it lavishly with a light blue Turkey carpet fifty feet long, and four-poster beds hung with gold and silver damask. The bed in which the Queen slept had blue curtains trimmed with gold and silver lace, with bed cover of peach and ash-coloured silk, possibly to flatter the Queen's colouring, and the walls were adorned with long mirrors which were then considered a luxury. Glass of any kind, in fact, was a luxury, the windows alone being quite marvellous; the pantries were stocked with glass dishes for cream, the rooms were lighted by candles in glass candlesticks. Thirty distinguished guests were invited to meet the Queen, including Sir Philip Sydney with his father and mother and their personal servants.

Dugdale has a lot to tell us about the entertainment of the Sovereign. He says that a special Discourse was printed called *The Princeley Pleasures of Kenilworth Castle* and he describes the fantastic spectacles that were arranged and which may seem to our sophisticated eyes, a little too fanciful for real enjoyment. For instance, upon arrival, the Queen was greeted by the sight of a floating island, on the moat, upon which:

clad in Silks, the Lady of the Lake and two Nymphs waiting on her, who made a Speech to the Q, in Meeter of the Antiquity and Owners of that Castle which was closed with Cornets & other loud Musick.

A bridge, twenty feet wide by sixty feet long, was built, on each side of which were erected a series of pedestals bearing gifts from the Gods; for instance, a Cage of Wild Fowl, by Silvanus; sundry Sorts of rare Fruits by Pomona; Corn by Ceres; Wine by Bacchus; Sea-Fish by Neptune; Habiliments of War by Mars; Musical Instruments by Phoebus and so on. Players came out from Coventry and played a piece called *Hocks-Tuesday;* there was Morris dancing, bear-baiting, a country Bride-ale, Fireworks, Italian tumblers and the Chase of a Savage man with Satyrs. In all, three hundred and twenty hogsheads of ordinary beer was drunk. The historian Laneham, who was included in the party, like a present-day journalist travelling with Royalty, made the observation that, during the whole visit, the great clock was stopped and rang not a note, standing the whole time at two o'clock, which was the usual banqueting hour; a small detail but one giving authenticity to a somewhat fabulous reportage.

Shakespeare was eleven when all this took place. Within a few miles of the festivities at Kenilworth, the world's greatest dramatist and poet was growing up and soaking in all the impressions of his youth. The piece that the Coventry players played before the Queen has passed into oblivion, but the first of Shakespeare's plays, which she saw at Lord Southampton's house in the Strand sometime between 1592 and 1596, *Love's Labours Lost* by the young up-and-coming *Johannes Factotum*, is still played for our delight at least once a year in one part of the world or another nearly four hundred years after it was written.

And so to Stratford for which, in spite of all his successes in London, Shakespeare's affection never seemed to diminish. In 1597 he bought New Place, built originally by the famous Sir Hugh Clopton, modernised it, and lived there for the last few years of his life. It was left to his daughter Susanna, wife of Dr John Hall, who in turn left it to her daughter Elizabeth, later Lady Barnard, who had no children. After her death it was sold and later came into the hands of a clergyman called Francis Gastrell who wickedly had the house demolished in 1759 after a dispute with regard to parish assessments for the maintenance of the poor. The people of Stratford were so disgusted by his behaviour that he left the town and some sixteen years later his widow sold the site; it is now laid out as a garden and museum.

It is said that Queen Henrietta Maria, wife of Charles I, entering the town with a considerable army of foot guards and cavalry in June 1643, stayed at New Place with her court for three weeks.

The great architect, Sir Hugh Clopton, a native of Stratford and Lord Mayor of London, built the great stone bridge, three hundred and seventy-six yards long, of fourteen arches, at his own expense in the reign of Henry VII. It has carried traffic across the Avon at Stratford for nearly five hundred years.

There are two bridges at Stratford, one the famous Clopton Bridge and the other a red brick bridge of ten arches and of considerable merit. Be sure you don't stare respectfully at the wrong one; the brick bridge was built in the Victorian era to carry the horse trams which went between Stratford and Shipston-on-Stour.

Clopton Bridge has had an iron footpath added on the upstream side and on the opposite side great clusters of pale green foliage and the red flowers of Valerian, in season, hang over to be reflected in the water below, growing in profusion between the cracks in the stone and from exactly nothing in the way of soil. There are now so many swans that they are being disposed of to any takers, or lent, rather, because swans are the property of the Crown and cannot be sold.

John Aubrey, the diarist, tells us that Shakespeare returned on a visit to his native town every year. How many, many times he must have crossed Clopton Bridge from the London-Oxford road! With how heavy a heart he must have travelled when his boy Hamnet, aged twelve, lay dying! Did he ever come with fierce resentment at having to leave, however temporarily, his full and busy life in the metropolis? Or did he come always with a feeling of relief that once more he was returning to his own people, to the ageing wife to whom he was attached; his sprightly daughters? Did he return with a gaggle of smart friends for the wedding of Suzannah to the brilliant and famous Dr John Hall? And at the end, did he come back, glad to be home once more, or did he know that it was his last journey, that he was come to Stratford never to leave it again, but to lay his bones beside the quietly flowing Avon for ever?

Anne Hathaway's Cottage, Shottery, Warwickshire

Anne Hathaway was the daughter of William Hathaway who died a year previous to her marriage to William Shakespeare. He had married, as his second wife, Joan Hathaway, who became the mother of three boys. After his death Anne, now twenty-six, lived on, it is assumed, at Hewlands Farm, now shown as 'Anne Hathaway's Cottage' with her stepmother and the boys. (See also page 35)

The present cottage stands on the edge of a wilderness of subtopia and seems to have little to do with the poet who would hardly have conducted his undoubtedly passionate courtship in that cramped space with three school boys and Anne's stepmother about.

Whatever may have been the truth about the marriage, it endured and the fact that, in his will, Shakespeare left his wife his 'second best bed' may have no ill-feeling behind it at all but may simply be because he knew that it was *her* bed and she found it more comfortable than any other.

The caustic remarks which Shakespeare makes about nagging women, such as the scolding Adriana in *The Comedy of Errors*, with her 'venom clamours', have been put down to his experience with a wife eight years older than himself. But there is no proof at all that she was anything but a loving, self-effacing Woman-in-the-Background. Her son-in-law, Dr John Hall, husband of Shakespeare's frisky daughter Suzannah, wrote a kindly Latin tribute for his mother-in-law's grave, referring to the life-giving milk of a maternal breast and praying for a glorious resurrection and ascent to the stars.

Photo: Kenneth Scowen

Shakespeare's Birthplace, Stratford-upon-Avon, Warwickshire

Shakespeare's father, John Shakespeare, mayor of Stratford in 1568, had other property in Henley Street but for many years it seems to have been considered that this is the birthplace. It would present a very different appearance at that time. There would be a morass of mud and dirt outside, where the pavement and road are now laid. The house would smell of people who were not able to wash thoroughly; wood-smoke would lurk amongs the beams and rafters to make the eyes smart; the old greenish glass would admit a depressing, filtered light. When Mrs Shakespeare was confined, did she herself fetch the buckets of water that she would require from the well, and heat them up in sooty kettles over the fire, or did she have a servant to help? Her first two babies had died in infancy and it was desperately important that this one should survive; when the baby was born, he was not carried into the garden to lie in a luxury pram in which he could spend the first days of his life, but wrapped tightly in swaddling clothes and put in bed beside his mother in the intolerably stuffy room.

However, he survived, this beloved poet-philosopher, the working of whose mind has entered into the warp and woof of our every-day lives.

Upstairs there are some interesting documents, such as a copy of the First Folio, and prints of the existing portraits. The Chandos portrait by Ozias Humphrey, was painted in 1783. In this the poet is shown with the same recession of hair above an egg-shaped forehead, full round eyes and what a woman novelist would call 'sensitive' nostrils. It is less formal than the other portraits, which were probably taken from life, and that may be why one likes it better, but as it was painted some hundred and fifty years after his death and there is no reason to suppose that it is as like him as the Droeshout portrait, in the Memorial Library, which was painted from life, so they say. The writer overheard a woman remark after a long look at the engravings: 'Funny-looking little man, wasn't he?'

Photo: Kenneth Scowen

Shakespeare Memorial Theatre, Stratford-upon-Avon, Warwickshire

This, the second theatre to stand on this site, was erected in 1932 to replace the old theatre, which had been built by a member of the Flower family, the Stratford brewers, in 1879 and burnt out in 1926. This modern building has great dignity and charm when seen at night with the lights reflected in the waters of the Avon. Clever use has been made of the site; the refreshment bars and the restaurant are built along the north bank overlooking the river on their south side. On summer evenings, during the intervals, you can stroll along the terrace with your drink and, leaning over, look down into the water whilst the swans come silently to see if you have anything for them to eat. In winter time, with a grey sky full of snow, pressing down upon the roof-tops and hard frost freezing the river rims, you can sit at a delightful luncheon in the restaurant and see the swans flying in with an awful clatter of wings, to land successfully upon the icy black water.

The Victorian wing of the old theatre, now the Memorial Library, Picture Gallery and Museum, was not destroyed in the fire and has been left more or less as it was with a corridor joining the main building in the form of an arch. This does not blend at all badly with the new part. The Library has a fine collection of over seven thousand Shakespeare reference books as well as the portrait from which Martin Droeshout made the engraving for the First Folio.

At the time of writing, in the entrance hall of the Picture Gallery, there is a marvellous surrealist portrait of Sir Lawrence Olivier, by Salvador Dali.

Photo: Kenneth Scowen

Old Tramway Bridge, Stratford-upon-Avon, Warwickshire

This charming bridge was built a few yards down river from the famous Clopton Bridge to carry the horse tramway from the Canal basin to Moreton-in-Marsh, with a branch to Shipston-on-Stour. The company, calling itself 'The Stratford and Moreton Railway Company', was incorporated in 1821 and the railway was opened on September 5th 1862, which was the coming-of-age of the son of one of the principal shareholders, Lord Redesdale; there was some celebration, with a jingle specially written for the occasion, the middle verse of which runs:

> *To see our iron railway*
> *It makes one's heart content*
> *To know what's saved in firing*
> *Will nearly pay our rent.*

The distance between the two termini was fifteen miles and, for half the journey, the line ran adjacent to the turnpike road; it was thus considered that steam traction was undesirable and it was horse drawn. At the rear of the train was a truck called a '*dandy cart*' to carry the horse down inclines. It has been stated by several reliable writers that the horses used for pulling trains of this type would get so accustomed to the procedure that, on reaching the top of a hill, before the descent started, they would unhitch themselves from the front, wait for the trucks to roll slowly past and then leap nimbly on to the '*dandy cart*' which had a specially constructed sloping gangway. Once safely aboard, the horse found the journey less uncomfortable if it settled on its haunches! The railway had a chequered history; at first it was not profitable but, in 1853, the gauge was changed and a passenger service operating twice daily was started. A journalist of the time highly praises the pleasure of the trip. He mentions the kind consideration of the driver who, before they entered tunnels, would suggest that those travelling outside would do well to remove their hats and duck their heads, and, on descending steep inclines, would apply the brakes as tightly as possible in order that the passengers could take a firm hold and so avoid being 'pitched off headforemost'. A truck used 'principally for goods', which ran until 1881, can still be seen preserved beside the bridge. The rails have been taken up and it is now a very pleasant walk along the old track, across the bridge and along the embankment. It would be a delightful day's walk to follow the track along its whole length, to Moreton-in-Marsh.

Photo: Camera Clix

Mary Arden's House at Wilmcote, Warwickshire

A great deal has been said and written about the grandness of the family to which Shakespeare's mother belonged. It is quite clear when one sees the house where she lived with her parents before she was married, that she came from yeomen who were 'well connected'.

This is a typical yeoman's dwelling, with two and a half bedrooms which were at one time reached by climbing a crude ladder. The floors are incredibly wavy and a great beam stretches across the middle of the room not more than four feet from the floor. On the ground floor are two rooms divided by a stone-flagged passage running from front to back of the house. In the summer these doors stand open so that one can see right through and out into the farmyard behind, with the pump within a few feet of the back door. Of the two ground-floor rooms with their great hearths, one was the living-room-kitchen and at the back, on the north side, is the buttery where all the dairy work was done. It has been much restored but is still a very charming house indeed in delightful surroundings.

The farm-buildings are seventeenth century and of great interest; many tools and old farm instruments are set out for those inclined to examine them. There is a huge stone cider press, for instance, an early fire engine and an old coach.

The dovecot, now splendidly clean, is impressive, with hundreds of nesting boxes built into the stone fabric of the walls.

Beside the station, on the way back to Stratford, you cross the delightful, but now disused, Stratford-Birmingham canal, its towing-path covered with grass.

Photo: Kenneth Scowen

Henley-in-Arden, Warwickshire

Now on one of the main roads into Birmingham, Henley-in-Arden was once as charming as its name. When the anxiety about being run over has been overcome, the mile-long street of houses in black-and-white and Tudor brick work may be greatly enjoyed. The old market cross used to be a centre of busy trading. In more isolated villages, these were often known as butter crosses because it was to this spot that the farmers' wives would bring their home-made butter and eggs, in covered baskets, for sale once or twice a week.

Henley is a good example of an autonomous town with its own Court Leet, or manor-court. 'There', Trevelyan explains, 'the affairs of the lord of the manor and his copyhold tenants were decided and registered, as well as the internal relations of the community of farmers of the open field and sharers of the common pasture and waste.' He goes on: 'The English villager had not only rights but functions in the society of which he was a member. Many were always very poor and some were victims of oppression, but there was a spirit of independence running through all classes under the old system of land-tenure before the eighteenth-century enclosures broke up the village community.'

The Guildhall where the Court Leet was held, still stands in a good state of repair with a fine old timbered roof. An example of the Great Seal of England under Henry VI can be seen, in green wax. The windows of the Guildhall overlook a little Dutch garden of the period with dwarf box hedges from which a glorious fragrance, so essentially English, rises after a shower of rain.

To the South of the church runs the stream called the Alne which divides Henley from its sister village of Beaudesert, (pronounced Belser locally). Roman remains have been found here and there was once a castle on the mound beyond, with a moat round it. The castle itself had disappeared even in Dugdale's time and was the stronghold of the Montfords, to be distinguished from the de Montforts, one of whom was Warden of the Welsh marches and closely connected with the crown. The church has been much restored but has some good examples of Saxon and Norman work in the chancel arch and doorway.

Photo: Kenneth Scowen

Welford-on-Avon, Warwickshire

This is a charming place. Here the Avon widens out, becoming a really beautiful river. Across the long bridge is an inn called 'The Four Alls' after a quaint old sign of four shadowy figures, now under cover in the porch:

The king who rules over all
The parson who prays for all
The soldier who fights for all
The farmer who pays for all

It may once have been called after the awl, a shoemaker's small tool and the verse made up by someone feeling particularly witty after a draught of the good ale.

There are some delightful cottages and the church has a genuine old lych gate. From the outside the church has a slightly unfamiliar look which is probably due to the mortar-work which has been plastered all over the stone fabric and yellow-washed, with a pleasantly unusual effect.

The life and vitality of the church seem to spring at you as soon as you enter. There are four shallow, low, bounding Norman arches in glorious honey-coloured stone forming arcades between the nave and the North and South aisles. A great bowl of flowers stands underneath a rather charming oil-planting of the Blessed Virgin with a quaintly elderly Child. There is a Jacobean pulpit and the oak rood screen is a War Memorial.

In a bottom corner of the East window is inset a tiny glass photograph of the son of one of the rectors, Basil Arthur Davis, a good-looking young man who was killed in a motor accident.

In a cul-de-sac, behind the church, is the old whitewashed Rectory, down a drive behind fine iron gates. Opposite is a gem of a small redbrick Queen Anne house.

Photo: Kenneth Scowen

The River and the seventeenth-century Bridge at Bidford, Warwickshire

Bidford was a Roman village a great many years before it became associated with the Shakespeare legend. Built on Rycknield, or Icknield Way, locally known as Buckle Street, it was probably a halting-place for Roman travellers from Gloucester to East Anglia. The Romans did not make new roads so much as re-make the old British trackways for use as military roads in the way the Americans have re-made a few of our farm lanes to provide adequate approaches to their great air-fields and missile bases. Following the Romans, the Church was responsible for the upkeep of roads and resting-places, and, in many cases, as at Bidford, the building of bridges. There was probably a monastic resting-place for travellers here long before the famous 'Falcon Inn'. Chaucer has much to tell us about the jolly travelling parties of medieval days and, on the whole, travelling seems to have been if not as comfortable, at least much more fun then than now.

This small town of stone and timber cottages and charming gardens, with a delightful view of the distant Cotswolds, had a reputation for exceptionally good ale and you can still get a very excellent brew at any of its half-dozen inns.

Nearby, a Saxon burial-ground was found with over two hundred graves containing the bodies of men with their weapons and women with their ornaments of crude bronze and gold jewellery, much of which can be seen at the museum in Stratford. It would seem that a pretty ruthless battle was once fought here, with men and women thrown hurriedly into the graves.

There are now boats for hire and a delightful afternoon can be spent paddling slowly on the river, under the arches of the bridge and alongside the meadow where the annual Fair is still held. (See also page 36)

Photo: Kenneth Scowen

Jephson Gardens, Leamington Spa, Warwickshire

Leamington Spa is a comparatively modern town which grew up in the hypochondriacal days of George IV round the mineral springs. The actor Macready, who sprang to fame in the parts of Richard III and King Lear, started the fashion for drinking and splashing about in the rather nasty water; and the town was made when the First Gentleman in England came over, whilst staying at Warwick Castle, to do the same. Dr Henry Jephson, the physician, had a great many wealthy and famous patients. Ruskin went to him for a check-up in 1843, and stayed forty-two days for a course of the waters, at the end of which the great doctor said: 'Sir, you may go, your health is in your own hands.' To which Ruskin remarks: 'Truly my health was in my own hands and I immediately reverted, in perfect health, to brown potatoes and cherry pie.' In the 'Authentic Edition' of *Dombey & Son* there is an enchanting illustration by 'Phiz' of Mr Dombey and the Major in the course of their stroll round Leamington, meeting Mrs Skewton and Mrs Granger: The Page, nearly as much aslant as his own shadow, was toiling after the chair, uphill, like a slow battering-ram.'

It is a charming town, stuccoed houses built in rows of infinite lightness, wrought-iron balconies, a Pump Room with squat Corinthian columns resembling those of Bath and all the grace and mannerisms of the Regency period.

The art of laying-out a public garden, in the Regency times, was comparatively new and Jephson Gardens must be one of the most successful efforts that the country can show. Clever use has been made of the slow-flowing river Leam and some excellent tree-planting took place. Gigantic holm-oaks (*Quercus*) abound; these splendid trees are evergreen and their average lifetime is a thousand years. The peace and charm of the gardens, however, is not enough to attract the modern sightseer in quantity; every Autumn the gardens are illuminated and a number of strangely transient 'attractions' have been added in the forms of two synthetic swans about six feet high; numerous groups of small coloured gnomes and dwarfs; a Mad-Hatter's tea party and a Gurgle-Glen; all greatly appreciated, to judge by the screams of laughter to be heard.

At a small chapel in Clemens Street, converted into a workshop in 1929, a staff of twenty-five pioneers started to make Lockheed brakes. They were successful and expanded so rapidly that now, in Tachbrook Road, Automotive Products have one of the finest modern factories in the country, covering acres of land, in pleasant surroundings, with only one tall chimney!

Photo: Kenneth Scowen

Exhall, Warwickshire

Though it announces itself enthusiastically at either end Exhall is hardly a place at all, but a few cottages and a tiny church on a road to nowhere. The cottage is less impressive than it looks in the picture; let into the front wall, as can be seen, is a well-head with an old-fashioned wooden roller and a broken rope; there is an iron handle but so close to the wall that it is difficult to turn it. On the other side of the road are two villas typical of their period; they are built in bright red brick in the Maidenhead-Edwardian style and are called 'Ivydene' and 'Sunnyside'. A hundred years hence people may come to look at them in admiration.

The small church was rebuilt in 1861 and a notice in the chancel naively says that the rebuilding 'obliterated its former ancient appearance'. Though it has a nave and chancel, it seems to have been built by an architect whose main interest lay in the building of non-conformist chapels. It has a pitch-pine dado all round, below walls distempered 'burnt Sienna' as it is called in a paint box. The pews, too, are varnished pitch pine which may possibly account for the curiously distinctive smell one gets in buildings of this kind. It is just a little bleak.

Photo: Black Star

Stoneleigh Abbey, Warwickshire

Stoneleigh should be approached from Leamington, through Stoneleigh Park, one of the loveliest stretches of wooded Warwickshire and part of the old Forest of Arden. Splendid old oaks still grow here in the deer park and there is one known as 'Shakespeare's Oak' under which, it is suggested, the Bard wrote *As You Like It*. Authors seldom, if ever, write out of doors, but, in this case, it may be that he was forced out of his narrow house into the wide open spaces a half-day's walk from the town to escape the noise made by Suzannah and the twins:

> *Unbridled children, grown*
> *Too headstrong for their mother.*

The wrestling scene takes place 'On the lawn before the Duke's Palace' and later, when the scene is the Forest of Arden, the Duke enters with Lords and Foresters: 'Are not these woods more free from peril than the envious court?' There follows the discourse on deer-hunting:

> *...Under an oak whose antique root peeps out*
> *Upon the brook that brawls along this wood:*
> *To which place a poor sequestered stag*
> *That from the hunter's aim had ta'en a hurt*
> *Did come to languish, and indeed, my lord,*
> *The wretched animal heaved forth such groans*
> *That their discharge did stretch his leathern coat*
> *Almost to bursting and the big round tears*
> *Coursed one another down his innocent nose*
> *In piteous chase; and this the hairy fool,*
> *Much marked of the melancholy Jaques,*
> *Stood on the verge of the swift brook,*
> *Augmenting it with tears.*

Did our poet, sitting musing under the oak, observe such a scene which roused his compassion so that when he returned home he rushed quill to paper on behalf of the 'poor sobbing deer'?

The material to be observed floating upon the surface of the river, in the photograph, is not broken ice but detergent. (See also page 44)

Photo: A. F. Kersting

Compton Wynyates, Warwickshire

The old pink brick-built house of Compton Wynyates grows straight out of the greenest of well-kept lawns at the bottom of a great airless bowl of silence. It was once entirely surrounded by a moat of which traces can be seen, still and lily-grown. The sides of the bowl are now covered with trees but were once vineyards, hence the name Wynyate, and the house was kept supplied with its own wine. There is a fine sharp echo from these hillsides which once repeated the sound of horses hooves and troops marching out across the drawbridge under the command of Spencer Compton, second Earl of Northampton, who raised at his own expense a division of the best disciplined men in the army, to fight for Charles I at Edge Hill, three miles away, in October 1642. Four years later the house was garrisoned by the Parliamentarians who demolished the old church, a few yards from the house, and the family memorials.

The church, however, was rebuilt at the Restoration and unspoilt by the recent restorer, it should not be missed. It is a rare mixture of Renaissance and Tudor Gothic with no chancel and a side pulpit. The box pews are light in colour. The ceiling paintings were in such bad condition that recently they have had to be plastered over, but the white plaster of ceiling and walls creates a lightness that shows to perfection the splendid extra large hatchments in all their restored glory. (Hatchments were large wooden tablets, square or diamond-shaped, used at funerals and painted with the armorial bearing of the deceased.)

If Compton Wynyates was an extremely noisy, bustling centre during the Civil Wars, it is the reverse now; the silence is almost oppressive and a bumble-bee crashing about in the vicinity draws more attention to itself than would a Boeing bomber overhead.

Photo: A. C. K. Ware

Kenilworth Castle, Warwickshire

That rollicking old story-teller, Sir Walter Scott, has woven around Kenilworth an enchanting story, so widely read that most people know a great deal more fiction about the castle than they do of the equally exciting facts. The astonishing disparity between this photograph and the plate, dated 1816, a reproduction of which appears in the front of the O.U.P. editions of *Kenilworth*, will give some idea of how fantastic Scott's Gothick (spelt with a k) novel is. It may be that the acute sense of disappointment on seeing the remains of the castle, picturesque though they are, arises from the difference between what one now sees and the wildly romantic illustrations to the book. Though Scott sticks fairly well to the description by the historians of the great reception given by the Earl of Leicester for the Queen, he introduces slap-stick whenever possible, as, for instance, when Flibbertigibbet sticks a pin into the gigantic behind of the huge hall porter just as he is about to receive the Sovereign.

In a footnote to the description of the party Scott says:

'See Laneham's *Account of the Queen's Entertainment at Kenilworth* in 1575, a very diverting tract written by as great a coxcomb as ever blotted paper.'

And to the description of Leicester handing the Queen up to the throne which was prepared for her Scott adds another footnote:

To justify what may be considered as a high-coloured picture, the author quotes the original of the courtly and shrewd Sir James Melville, being then Queen Mary's envoy in London. 'I was required,' says Sir James, 'to stay till I had seen him made Earl of Leicester, and Baron of Denbigh, with great solemnity; herself (Elizabeth) helping to put on his ceremonial, he sitting on his knees before her keeping great gravity and discreet behavior; but she could not refrain from putting her hand to his neck to kittle (i.e. tickle) him, smilingly, the French Ambassador and I standing beside her'.

There is in existance an epitaph on the famous Earl of Leicester which reads:

Here lies a valiant warrior,
Who never drew a sword;
Here lies a noble courtier
Who never kept his word;
Here lies the Erle of Leister,
Who govern'd the estates,
Whom the earth could never living love,
And the just heaven now hates.

72

Photo: Barnabys Ltd

Worcester Cathedral

Like Notre Dame, the effect of Worcester Cathedral is greatly enhanced by its position, on the banks of a wide, slowly-flowing river. It is built of soft red sandstone with the curious blueish overtones indigenous to the land, a material which does not withstand the ravages of time.

A King of England is buried here, though not one of our best, King John, who died at Newark and ordered that his body should be laid at Worcester beside the quiet Severn. The recumbent figure, the earliest royal sculptured figure in England, lies on a carved altar tomb with panels of the Royal arms. The colour has worn away, leaving only the grey granite. As was the custom in those early days, the body was salted and wrapped in an ox-hide, in some cases gilded, and laid in a stone coffin. The last of the Angevin Kings was dressed in his royal robes and for luck they put upon his head a monk's cowl, so that he might slip unnoticed through Purgatory.

> *And they who to be sure of Paradise*
> *Dying put on the weeds of Dominic,*
> *Or in Franciscan thought to pass disguised.*

Leaving no stone unturned that might aid the old sinner, they buried him between the sainted bodies of St Oswald and St Wulstan. Morbid curiosity, or perhaps a better reason, caused them to open the grave in 1797; the body was found in a state of marvellous preservation and identified as being, without a doubt, that of John, King of England and Normandy, 1199 to 1216.

The Cathedral has many interesting monuments and memorials to the famous men and women of the city and is the proud possessor of three Colours of the Scots Guards which went through the wars with Wellington to the Battle of Waterloo and were given by the Iron Duke to Sergeant-Major Good, who died in 1850.

More often than not, plain white marble seems lifeless and out of place in our old stone cathedrals. But this is one of the few occasions when Victorian sculpture has produced a miracle of beauty in the figure of Bishop Philpott, by Sir Thomas Brock. It is beautifully placed and the soft light falling on the grave features and raised hand are strangely moving. (See also page 31)

Photo: A. F. Kersting

Pershore Abbey, Worcestershire

The great Benedictine Abbey of Pershore has had a number of dedications. At present it is dedicated to the Holy Cross and in earlier times its patrons were SS Mary, Peter and Paul. Earlier still, it was known as SS Mary and Ædburga, the latter being the saintly grand-daughter of Alfred the Great who, when asked by her father as a child whether she would prefer, as a birthday gift, jewels, toys or a book of the Gospels, chose the Gospels. She entered a nunnery and died in 960 AD. Some of her bones were brought to Pershore where they were placed in a gilt coffin and attracted many pilgrims.

The structure of the Abbey Church had been greatly altered; little remains of the original, but Early English work in the Choir arcade is of considerable rarity and beauty and has been called one of the best examples in the country. Excavations have shown that the original nave was very similar to that of Tewkesbury, – Romanesque, with massive round piers, – and was probably built about the same time. The bell tower has an exceedingly beautiful lantern storey and there is a peal of eight bells, amongst the finest in the country. The pinnacles of the tower are the work of Gilbert Scott.

One of the Abbots, Thomas Upton (1379) was drowned crossing the Avon, after which disaster the monks built the bridge, still to be seen. Amongst the interesting monuments is the Haselwood Tomb, late sixteenth century. The arched recess once contained two kneeling figures, now vanished. Their ten children remain below, carved in relief, three boys, six girls and the baby in the cradle. All kneel in faithful prayer except the crazy mixed-up one who stands turned forward, laughing.

The effigy of the Knight Templar is interesting (*circa* 1250) in that he holds a horn in his right hand, which may be evidence that the Knight held his land by cornage tenure of 'horn geld', and at his feet is a hare from which it has been deduced that his name was Hareley. It is thought to be the figure of Sir William de Harley, Lord of Harley in Shropshire who fought in the first Crusade and was knighted by Godfrey de Bouillon at Jerusalem. (See also page 24)

76

Photo: Hugh Sibley

Chaddesley Corbett, Worcestershire

As lovely, in its way, as any Cotswold village, it differs in that the whole country-side, twenty or so miles west of Stratford, and on the very edge of the Black Country, is different. The earth here is the colour of plant pots and great oaks and ashes decorate the still wonderful countryside. The village is tiny and not one house or cottage is without interest. There is a genuine, honest-to-goodness old, and not *Olde*, post-office-cum-shop, its only concession to modernity being a cooled glass-fronted counter for perishable food. It has just the right old village shop smell. The church is quite different from those to the south and east; it is built of that pinkish stone, so blurred and soft that the texture looks to be that of marshmallows. It has a fine spire and a lovely modern East window. There is a pinkish Norman font and the oldest brass in the county, that of the de Forests, 1511. This is the only church in England dedicated to St Cassian and nobody seems to know quite which one, the Roman, the French or the Greek.

There can be no more lovely Elizabethan manor to be seen for half-a-crown than Harvington Manor, a mile from here. It belongs to the Catholic Archdiocese of Birmingham and the land round to the National Trust. The walls rise directly out of the moat, the sun-soaked, soft red brickwork might have been painted by Vermeer. It is utterly quiet, occasionally a yellow leaf drops silently as dew on to the still water. The house was built in Tudor times by Humphry Pakington and has been untouched since 1700. There are some notable murals (1577), the best examples of Elizabethan domestic wall decoration in England. The treads under the newel staircase show the old decoration and in the tiny chapel the walls are painted with red and white drops, of blood and tears, emblems of The Passion. The house has always had strong Catholic associations; the Franciscan missionary, now known as Blessed John Wall (not to be confused with Dr Wall of Worcester) was the Chaplain here and the last of the English martyrs to be burnt for his Faith. He was one of twenty who suffered a cruel death 'which he faced with the utmost sanctity' at Worcester in 1679. The house contains a *true copy* of his speech on the scaffold. In a room at moat level you sit and have tea with the scent of the fresh rushes picked from the moat, lying on the stone floors, as they have been laid for nearly four centuries, and you can feed the swans from the windows.

Photo: The British Travel and Holidays Association

Great Comberton, Worcestershire

This is the type of cottage seen in all the villages which cluster round the base of the oval hump of Bredon Hill: Kemerton, Beckford, Bredon's Norton, Overbury, Elmley Castle, the Combertons, Ashton-under-Hill, Conderton: mainly thatched and half-timbered, they are different in style from the stone-built, stone-tiled dwellings of the Cotswolds. Connoisseurs prefer this tiny, unspoilt part of England to any; others find it altogether too sweet.

With one or two famous exceptions, no labourer's cottages survive which were built before the end of the seventeenth century; the mediaeval 'council houses' the huts for the labourers of Shakespeare's day, were so crudely-built that they have perished. A cottage such as this one at Great Comberton was almost certainly an overseer or husbandman's house, and not a labourer's hut.

Manorial surveys seldom describe cottages but the Hearth Tax Assessments give us some idea of the size; the majority of people lived in houses with only one hearth at the end of the seventeenth century, and this hearth would burn wood and charcoal. Coal, which came by sea from Tyneside and was thus called sea-coal, at that period, was almost unknown in inland places.

Surviving maps and plans of an early date show villages and groups of cottages where none now exist. Some were abandoned during the Black Death and innumerable cottages were swept away by the Enclosures Acts; as roads and transport improved, the people moved, for expediency, towards the highway. The villages round Bredon, however, have been the chosen dwelling places for people since the Iron Age. They seem to nestle against the hill on one side for protection and on the other side they have the rich land watered by the Avon with its splendid orchards and growing-soil unequalled anywhere in England, other than in Kent.

Photo: Kenneth Scowen

The Old Fleece, Bretforton, Worcestershire

This tiny, famous Inn was painted by Sargeant; scrupulously kept and always gay with quite exceptional flower-decoration, it is entirely unspoilt and has been a meeting-place for the people of the Vale of Evesham for hundreds of years.

Bretforton itself is an interesting village; once the property of the Abbey of Evesham, the Norman cellar of the Abbey grange, or farmhouse, still remains, with the fish-pond which supplied the monks with fresh fish and the dovecot which gave them pigeon flesh. Many of the families from which local people are now proud to trace their descent were yeomen; some of these yeomen were descended from feudal families and others came into existence at the Reformation, either when they were given land by the Government or acquired it by private annexation, and Bretforton is a good example of the small town of the yeomen of Shakespeare's day because the Manor was broken up and sold to the tenants. There are a number of fine middle-class houses. The prosperity of these householders is shown by the large dovecots which they possessed. Bretforton has six, big enough to hold from a thousand to two thousand pigeons.

The church is worth seeing, with an ancient font, in use for eight hundred years, a box pew, Jacobean panelling brought from Stratford, fragments of mediaeval glass and some whimsical carving. The local Boy Who Made Good came from the family of Hewins. Many of these boys became priests but one of them rose to be Chartered Accountant, or Auditor, as it was then called, to the Court of Queen Katherine of Aragon. Another, who died in 1545, left a widow who married Shakespeare's grand-father on the Arden side and became the poet's 'step-grandmother'.

This village is well worth a visit; it lies a little off the beaten track, quiet, peaceful; on a warm spring morning there can be few pleasures to equal that of sitting in the cool of one of 'The Fleece's' several parlours, drinking a pint of shandy, while the sun streams in across the now spotlessly clean stone-flagged floors on to which, long before Shakespeare's time, the local philosophers spat as they held forth.

Photo: Kenneth Scowen

Fladbury Ferry, Worcestershire

If you are nice to the ferryman, you can have fun pulling yourself across this smooth mill pond, in a huge punt, by a steel hawser fixed from bank to bank, whilst the fish pop their heads out of the water.

Fladbury is quite a considerable village which, one feels, has been the chosen settlement of people for many hundreds of years. There is a Saxon burial ground nearby. But progress seems to have swept through on the way elsewhere, leaving odd traces. The Victorian school has an addition right up to the minute, adjoining it; and on a triangular scrap of grass, in the centre of which there really should be an old butter cross, is a tall concrete lamp post. A few yards away there is a charming cast iron one. A tall, thin Dickensian-type of Georgian brick house has been painted cream and white to resemble timber-framing and is called 'Ice Bar' and hiding behind it is a cottage with the quaint name of 'Pippins'.

The church has many things of interest. It is the burial place of William Lloyd, father of one of the Rectors. The father was one of the 'Immortal Seven' who, in the reign of James II, stood trial with six others after imprisonment in the Tower, for insidious popery. They were all acquitted amid scenes of wild rejoicing and Lloyd became Bishop of Lichfield, and later of Worcester. He lived to the age of ninety but towards the end seems to have become slightly unbalanced, declaring himself able to foretell the future.

There is a window in the church with the old glass brought from Evesham Abbey at the Dissolution and showing the arms of six knights who were killed in the battle of Evesham. The lion in the arms of Simon de Montfort seems oddly similar to that on the Charlett Memorial on the North wall. Two small brasses commemorate two incumbents, Plewme (1504) and Mardon (1458), and there is a splendid brass of John and Eleanor Throckmorton (1445). They seem to have been the great great-great-grandparents of the Sir Nicholas Throckmorton after whom Throckmorton Street in London is named.

Photo: Black Star

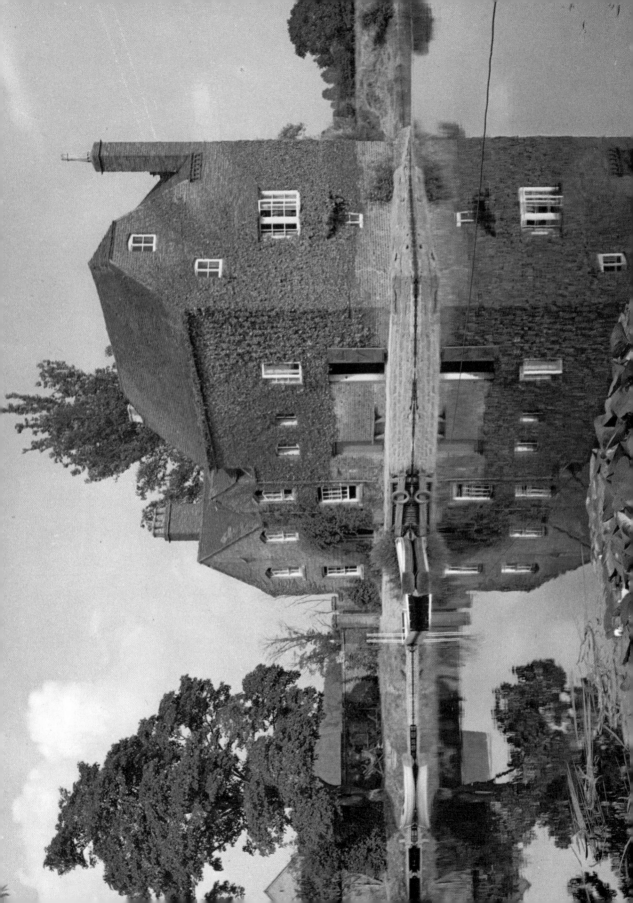

Broadway, Worcestershire

In the Worcestershire Domesday the reference to Broadway reads in free translation: 'This same church (Pershore) holds BRADEWEIA. There are xxx hides paying geld. In demesne are iii ploughs and a priest and xlvi villeins with xxii ploughs; there are viii serfs. Total T.R.E. (*Tempore regis Edwardi*) was worth xii*li*. x*s*, it is now worth xiv*li*. x*s*. Of this same land a freeman held in T.R.E. ii hides and a half which he bought of Abbot Edmund; this land was in demesne. There are now ii ploughs in the demesne of the Abbot for his food supply. It was and is worth xxx *s*. This land Urso claims as the gift of the King and says he exchanged it for a manor which was in the demesne.'

The present villeins, or country labourers, are very fine craftsmen indeed, workers in wood and first-class cabinet makers. At a small factory they turn out some of the best hand-made modern furniture in the country and this is exported all over the world. Eastern potentates sit on chairs and desks made at Broadway in England and examples of this very fine furniture can be found in important banks, palaces and offices everywhere.

The early village of Broadway formerly clustered round the charming old church of Saint Ædburga and has gradually shifted itself a mile or so Northward to the main London-Worcester road. No cottages remain at the old site but numerous houses for the prosperous overseers were built along the road, now forming a mile-long village-street of great charm. The new church was built in the first half of the last century on the site of the old Chapel of Ease; though plain and uncompromising in style, the stone of which it is built has that quality of constant change, which is the essence of true beauty and can suddenly, as, for example, on a stormy winter evening, spring to life in a blaze of glorious colour which is staggering. Broadway had a quaint old custom of paying to the vicar one penny, per person, per annum for the upkeep of the church. This has now lapsed. (See also page 9)

Photo: R. J. Westlake

Landscape near Stow-on-the-Wold, Gloucestershire

It has been said that the countryside is probably more deserted now than it was when it was a Saxon jungle and certainly a good deal more than in Shakespeare's day. At first thought this may seem absurd but, upon consideration, the observation refers to such countryside as is left, not to the acres of new suburbs and the grass verges of the roads which are thick with picknickers. The time spent by the farmer upon his land has been greatly decreased since the old Saxon eight-ox plough drove its laborious way through the heavy clay. Moreover, this part of the island was seriously affected by the Enclosure Acts when they began to take effect. Under the new legislation, the strips of land owned by the peasants were appropriated and fenced in, the peasant being compensated by a small sum of money which he promptly dissipated in drink. After the Restoration, there was an ever-increasing movement to accumulate land in large compact estates and some of the great political peers became owners of enormous tracts of country. Terrible hardships were suffered by the peasants and small landowners. It is estimated that over two million men were swept from the land by the march of progress; it was left to the wind and the sky and the occasional tractor.

From Stow-on-the-Wold, looking in any direction, one can see great stretches of wonderfully rich growing country, now in private ownership. It can easily be understood that the appearance of the land has improved considerably; no doubt at one time it had a slightly allotment-like look. Here and there is a herd of beautifully-kept Friesians, an occasional flock of sheep and, sometimes, a man. No longer does one see the stooping figures that Millet painted; instead a sturdy plywood creature, armed to the teeth, in a jacket painted a startling luminous rock-and-roll orange, seems to stride across the fields: the new type of scarecrow.

Here, in the Cotswolds, as in Essex, are made straw 'dollies'. They are beautifully constructed straw figures and mobiles, the method of making which has been handed down from generation to generation since pagan times. Often they are made for Harvest Festivals and as often to top the stack, for luck; it is probable that they are of profane rather than sacred origin.

Photo: John Tarlton

The Church, Chipping Campden, Gloucestershire

Chipping Campden is a grey-gold wool town lying almost hidden in a hollow in a fold of the Cotswold hills. Like all the wool towns, it has a splendid church and the town possesses many fine large houses in its wide, quiet main street.

The historian Cox says that the Saxon Kings in the Heptarchy met in this town (A.D. 689) to consult about making war and peace with the Britons. The manor was held before the Conquest by Earl Harold; in due course it passed to the Crown and was granted by Elizabeth I to Sir Thomas Smith whose descendants built the great house which was destroyed at the time of the Civil Wars by the Royalist troops after the King's visit, as a precaution against it being occupied by the Parliamentarians. The market was famous for its stockings. The historian seems to have been impressed by Chipping Campden's provision for its poor, which appears to have been considerable. Sir Baptist Hicks built almshouses for six poor men and six poor women and endowed them with Three-and-Fourpence to be given weekly to each person, besides an allowance for a black Gown and Coals. He also gave '500 *l.* for a Stock to set the Poor at Work'. Further: 'There are so many Gifts for Bread in this Parish, to be disposed weekly to the Poor, *viz* six Dozen every Sunday, besides two and forty Pounds and ten Shillings a Year to be expended in Bread for them at Discretion, that there seems not to be any Place that has better Provision in this kind, both against Want and Dearnes of Corn'. Thus did the people of Chipping Campden live without the Welfare State in the seventeenth century.

Trevelyan, in his *English Social History*, says that the town has 'the most beautiful village street now left in the island: for Chipping Campden was not an ordinary Gloucestershire village but a collecting centre for England's greatest trade'.

Photo: Kenneth Scowen

The Mill, River and Abbey at Tewkesbury, Gloucestershire

The early history of Tewkesbury is enlivened by continual reference to the brothers Oddo and Doddo, two rich noblemen who, as an act of piety, are reputed to have founded the monastery to the glory of God on their own estate near the Severn at a place where a certain hermit called Theocus – *'unde Theokusburia '*– had made his abode. Some historians dismiss Oddo and Doddo as legendary and state that there was a town at Tewkesbury in the days of prehistory. Others believe that it is a town of Anglo-Saxon foundation and called 'Dukes' Bury' from the Dukes Oddo and Doddo. In the Register of Tewkesbury, there is a picture of the two knights each holding a tiny model of a church and standing under a pomegranate tree. It is not known where they lie buried but at Deerhurst, a few miles away, they show an old tomb bearing the inscription: 'Duke Dodo caused this royal palace to be consecrated as a church to the honour of the Virgin Mary on account of the love which he bore to his brother Almeric.'

During the wars between the English and the invading Danes, it seems that the abbey was twice destroyed by fire, Tewkesbury being part of the battleground on which the issue was fought out under the leadership of Alfred the Great, the last crowning victory being won by the English King at Boddington, a few miles away, between the Severn and the Wye in A.D. 893.

The present Abbey Church was consecrated on November 20th 1123. In the midst of the nave, on a few square yards of pavement, the Bishop of Worcester wrote the alphabet twice with the end of his pastoral staff, first in Greek letters from the North-east to the South-west and then in Latin from the South-east to the North-west, in the form of a cross.

The Benedictine Monastery broke up in 1539 but the small town which had grown up round it continued in prosperity, lying, as it does, on extremely fertile soil. Like so many of the towns in this part of the country, it had its share of affluence in the clothing trade and in Shakespeare's day did a thriving business in mustard. A person wearing a particularly sour expression was described as having 'lived on Tewkesbury mustard' and Shakespeare (2 *Henry IV*) says: 'His wit's as thick as Tewkesbury mustard.'

Cox, in his *History of Glocestershire* states that: 'the Cloathing Trade thrives here, being encouraged by its Nearness to Cotswold-Hills and Stroud-Water; but the Mustard-Balls made here, so proper for clearing the Head, make it more talked of, tho' less profitable.' (See also page 26).

Photo: Kenneth Scowen

Summer Evening at Stanton, Gloucestershire

The hamlet of Stanton is situated a mile from the Cheltenham-Stratford road on the Western slopes of the North Cotswolds. In his *History of Glocestershire*, Cox makes no great mention of Stanton other than to state that it was situated in the old Kistegate Hundred and 'all the Children here taught, and several of them cloathed by part of an ancient Benefaction'.

A 'Tour of the Cotswolds' seldom omits this delightful little place and great coaches nose their way slowly down the narrow lanes so that people may have a quick look before going on to Broadway for tea. But Stanton is not a show-place in the way Broadway is; there is no room for a coach to park and nowhere for a large number of people to have tea.

Stanton Court is an E-shaped Elizabethan mansion built in glorious golden stone. The church, in the same stone, is cruciform with a spire and an excellent South window in the Perpendicular style, with traces of old glass. There is a Jacobean Communion table and a curious roundel, or medallion, taken from the ceiling and re-set in the South wall. It depicts a bird with the inscription 'Mauritus Raybury Loyer' written round the border. 'Loyer' is not a name, nor a profession, but a French word meaning landowner or owner of property.

The village has been lovingly preserved and the Manor House, the oldest house in the village, to be distinguished from Stanton Court, is a charming house in the main street, if so quiet a street can be so-called. This is now one of those delightful antique shops of the kind occupied by a family who live with and use the furniture for sale, where you can snatch up the coveted piece from under their very noses and go away rejoicing.

Photo: Kenneth Scowen

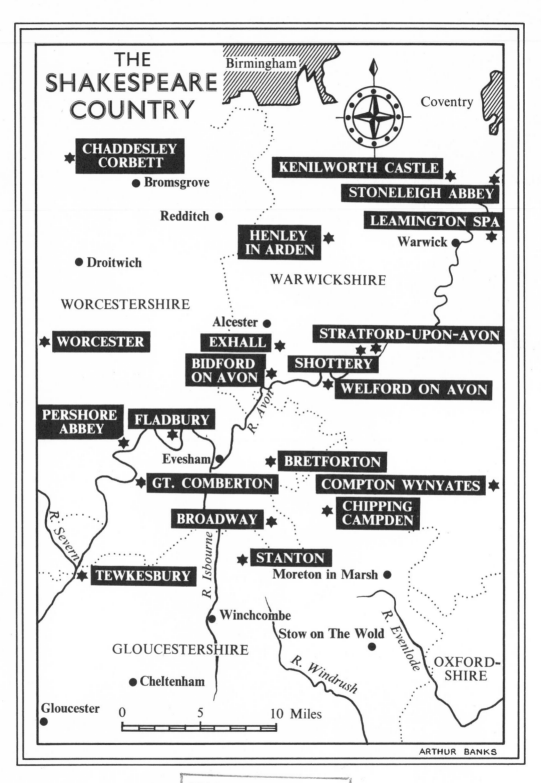

THE
SHAKESPEARE
COUNTRY

Birmingham

Coventry

CHADDESLEY
CORBETT

KENILWORTH CASTLE

● Bromsgrove

STONELEIGH ABBEY

Redditch ●

LEAMINGTON SPA

HENLEY
IN ARDEN

Warwick ●

● Droitwich

WARWICKSHIRE

WORCESTERSHIRE

Alcester ●

STRATFORD-UPON-AVON

WORCESTER

EXHALL

SHOTTERY

BIDFORD
ON AVON

WELFORD ON AVON

R. Avon

PERSHORE
ABBEY

FLADBURY

Evesham ●

BRETFORTON

GT. COMBERTON

COMPTON WYNYATES

BROADWAY

CHIPPING
CAMPDEN

R. Severn

R. Isbourne

STANTON

TEWKESBURY

Moreton in Marsh ●

Winchcombe ●

Stow on The Wold ●

R. Evenlode

GLOUCESTERSHIRE

R. Windrush

OXFORD-
SHIRE

● Cheltenham

Gloucester   0   5   10 Miles
●

ARTHUR BANKS